*This book is lovingly dedicated
to Kathy, Ben, and Becky—
three loves of my life who
have impacted me far more than
they can ever imagine*

CHARLES H. DYER

Under President Saddam Hussein, one of the world's most legendary cities has begun to rise again. More than an archaeological venture, the new Babylon is self-consciously dedicated to the idea that Nebuchadnezzar has a successor in Mr. Hussein, whose military prowess and vision will restore to Iraqis the glory their ancestors knew when all of what is now Iraq, Syria, Lebanon, Jordan, Kuwait, and Israel was under Babylonian control.

JOHN BURNS, *New York Times International,* October 11, 1990

He is a dangerous man possessing the world's most dangerous weapons. It is incumbent upon freedom-loving nations to hold him accountable, which is precisely what the United States of America will do.

PRESIDENT GEORGE W. BUSH, State of the Union address, January 29, 2002

Saddam has used chemical weapons, not only against an enemy state, but against his own people. Intelligence reports make clear that he sees the building up of his WMD [weapons of mass destruction] capability, and the belief overseas that he would use these weapons, as vital to his strategic interests, and in particular his goal of regional domination.

PRIME MINISTER TONY BLAIR, Foreword to British Government Dossier on Iraq, September 24, 2002

On the day the LORD gives you relief . . . you will take up this taunt against the king of Babylon: How the oppressor has come to an end! How his fury has ended! The LORD has broken the rod of the wicked, the scepter of the rulers, which in anger struck down peoples with unceasing blows, and in fury subdued nations with relentless aggression.

ISAIAH 14:3–6

CHARLES H. DYER

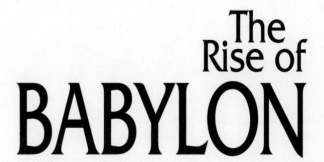

The
Rise of
BABYLON

IS IRAQ AT THE CENTER OF THE FINAL DRAMA?

MOODY PUBLISHERS
CHICAGO

© 1991, Revised 2003 by
CHARLES H. DYER

ISBN: 0-8024-0905-9

3 5 7 9 10 8 6 4 2

Printed in the United States of America

CONTENTS

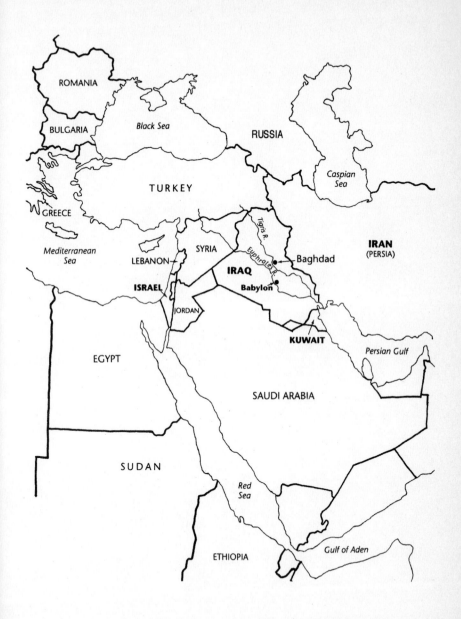

1
Babylon: Rising from the Ashes of Time

The dry, blistering heat was oppressive, and the last thing I wanted to do was hike alone along a sandy road and scale a dusty wall. But I had traveled from my home in Texas to Babylon, Iraq, and now that I was here, nothing short of an armed guard would stop me from exploring the ruined city that had always fascinated me.

Finally I was alone, for the moment, in a city that was nearly as old as civilization itself. Perhaps I was standing a few feet from the spot where Alexander the Great died or where Nebuchadnezzar once mused over the greatness of the city he had built. Maybe the young prisoner Daniel had absently run his fingers along this very wall and wished that he were back home in Jerusalem. Or perhaps somewhere in the sand under my feet was a fragment of the symbol of man's rebellion against God, the Tower of Babel.

I snapped several pictures of this bleak, undeveloped section of ruins and then slipped back over the wall to join the official party of foreigners of which I was a part. Saddam Hussein had invited us to Iraq for a cultural festival, to see the beauty of the new Babylon that was rising from the ruins. Like the other visitors, I clapped and smiled for my hosts at the appropriate times. But something arose from within my soul—a feeling part thrill, part chill.

The Bible forecasts the rebuilding of Babylon, and here, before my eyes, was another thrilling proof that Bible prophecies are infallible. But the Bible also reveals that the rebuilt Babylon will be brutally and suddenly destroyed with such force that not even one stone will ever be used again.

I looked down at the Babylonian ruins and saw twenty-five-hundred-year-old bricks that were ordered into place by Nebuchadnezzar. Over the centuries, thousands of his bricks have been taken out of the rubble and used to build nearby villages. Today the rebuilders of Babylon are laying additional bricks inscribed, "Rebuilt in the era of our President Saddam Hussein." These bricks, too, should last through the ages. What act of destruction could prevent their reuse?

Nuclear war, perhaps. But the Cold War is a fading memory. The United States and the other civilized nations of the world have never been more eager for peace and disarmament. Then my eyes fell upon a chilling twenty-foot portrait of Saddam Hussein, the self-described Knight of the Arab World, a man whom some call "the Butcher of Baghdad."

What does the future hold for Babylon? I wondered. *Whatever terrors lie ahead, they are sure to affect the entire world.*

Everything Old Is News Again

"Extra! Extra! Read all about it! Madman from Mesopotamia threatens the stability of the Middle East! World prepares for war!"

Are these headlines from today's *New York Times,* or are they the cries of a prophet who lived twenty-five-hundred years ago? History, it seems, is repeating itself. Descriptions of Iraq's threat to world peace today parallel descriptions of Nebuchadnezzar's rise to power in 605 B.C. Once again, the eyes of the world are riveted on the Middle East and the threat of one man. Once again, the world is painfully aware of Babylon.

At the heart of the current crisis is Saddam Hussein, president of Iraq. Well-known for atrocities, tortures, and ruthlessness, he seems bizarre and unreasonable to Western minds. What are his plans and ambitions? What relationship do his actions have with biblical prophecies and God's plans for the world? Is Saddam Hussein a link to Armageddon, or is he only the latest bead on a long string of would-be world conquerors? Hussein has baffled both his own countrymen and

Western foreign policy analysts.

While the world struggles to penetrate the enigma of Saddam Hussein, we can find an important, God-given clue in the Bible. *The key to the mystery of Saddam Hussein is Babylon.* From Genesis to Revelation, Babylon occupies a unique position in God's Word. Today the once-dead city is being revived by Saddam Hussein, who seeks to establish and lead an international power paralleling the glory of ancient Babylon.

Parade of Pride and Power

It is a cloudless September summer night, and the moon casts its shining image on the banks of the gentle Euphrates River. Thousands of guests and dignitaries walk by torchlight to Babylon's Procession Street and enter the city from the north. Instructed to line the streets along the massive walls, the guests obediently follow orders. When the audience is in place, the dark-eyed man in charge nods, and the procession begins.

Rows and rows of soldiers parade in, dressed in Babylonian tunics and carrying swords, spears, and shields. Interspersed among the ranks of soldiers are groups of musicians playing harps, horns, and drums. Clusters of children carry palm branches, and runners bear bowls of incense. Then come soldiers and still more soldiers in a seemingly endless line of men and weapons. After the procession, the guests attend a ceremony paying tribute to Ishtar, the mother goddess of Babylon.

Have I just described a scene of pagan worship from

the time of Daniel? Perhaps, but it is also exactly what I witnessed when I returned to Babylon a second time to attend the International Babylon Festival held under the patronage of Saddam Hussein.

Imagine, if you will, a ruler determined to stamp his name on the pages of history. His goal is complete dominion of all surrounding nations, and he has spent vast sums of money to outfit an army capable of carrying out his wishes. He holds absolute power, and he does not hesitate to execute those who pose even a remote threat to his leadership. People have been arrested and imprisoned for the simple crime of not revering his image.

Yet his military might is not his only claim to fame. He also sees himself as a patron of culture: of poets, artists, and architects. Even the bricks in Babylon bear his name as the personal overseer of its construction.

Is this a fair description of Saddam Hussein? Yes, but it also accurately describes Nebuchadnezzar II, the Babylonian king whose empire once stretched from sea to sea. In his day, the lands of what are now Iraq, Saudi Arabia, Syria, Lebanon, Jordan, Israel, and Kuwait were all under Babylonian control. In August 1990, Saddam Hussein tried to reclaim a portion of that early empire when he invaded Kuwait. A coalition of nations, led by the United States, pushed back the Iraqi army, but Hussein remained in control of Iraq. Could he still ever hope to reclaim the entire kingdom of Nebuchadnezzar?

The Bible Predicts a Reborn Babylon

Because Babylon was built in ancient times, and was a great city, it must be a great city again in the time of our new great leader, Saddam Hussein.

SHAFQA MOHAMMED JAAFAR, Babylon's chief archaeologist[1]

Babylon will be a great city again. The Bible mentions Babylon over two hundred and eighty times, and many of those references are to the future city of Babylon that is rising from the fine sands of the desert today. Consider the following biblical prophecies:

> *Babylon, the jewel of kingdoms, the glory of the Babylonians' pride, will be overthrown by God like Sodom and Gomorrah.*
> ISAIAH 13:19

Babylon was never suddenly overthrown like Sodom and Gomorrah in their fiery destruction. It was conquered by the Medes and Persians and fell into decline, but it was not violently destroyed.

> *An oracle concerning Babylon that Isaiah son of Amoz saw: . . . Wail, for the day of the LORD is near; it will come like destruction from the Almighty.*
> ISAIAH 13:1, 6

"The day of the LORD" described by Isaiah refers to the tribulation period that is still to come. Babylon's destruction, then, will come in the time of the Tribulation—a short period of time just before the second coming of Christ.

The LORD will have compassion on Jacob; once again he will choose Israel will and settle them in their own land. . . . They will make captives of their captors and rule over their oppressors. On the day the LORD gives you relief from suffering and turmoil and cruel bondage, you will take up this taunt against the king of Babylon: How the oppressor has come to an end! How his fury has ended! . . . All the lands are at rest and at peace; they break into singing.
ISAIAH 14:1–4, 7

When Babylon is ultimately destroyed, Israel will finally be at peace and will dwell in safety. Israel has been a nation since 1948, but not for one day has the nation of Israel known real peace or ease. It has never been able to claim all the lands God promised the Israelites, and Israel's Arab neighbors have been a constant threat and danger.

The House Built for Wickedness

Then the angel who was speaking to me [Zechariah] came forward and said to me, "Look up and see what this is that is appearing."

I asked, "What is it?"

He replied, "It is a measuring basket." And he added, "This is the iniquity of the people throughout the land."

Then the cover of lead was raised, and there in the basket sat a woman! He said, "This is wickedness," and he pushed her back into the basket and pushed the lead cover down over its mouth.

*Then I looked up—and there before me were two
women, with the wind in their wings! They had wings like
those of a stork, and they lifted up the basket between heaven
and earth.*

*"Where are they taking the basket?" I asked the angel
who was speaking to me.*

*He replied, "To the country of Babylonia to build a house
for it. When it is ready, the basket will be set there in its
place."*

ZECHARIAH 5:5–11

Zechariah was a product of the Babylonian exile of
the Jews in the sixth century before Christ. Born in
Babylon, he returned to Jerusalem in 538 B.C. Zechariah
was from a priestly family, and he watched his people
begin to rebuild the temple in 536 B.C.

The work in Jerusalem languished, however, and
God spoke to Zechariah and Haggai and called them to
deliver his message to the people: Rebuild the temple!
While this was their immediate message, God also gave
them a glimpse of His future plans for the nation of
Israel.

Zechariah had this vision about Babylon on February 15, 519 B.C. He saw a measuring basket, with a
cover, that was said to contain "the iniquity of the people throughout the land." The woman Zechariah saw
was wickedness personified, as though all the evil
deeds and actions done by humanity were represented
by one character. The heavy lead cover was designed to
keep the woman, or wickedness, from escaping.

After showing Zechariah this scene, the angel

pushed the woman into the basket and shut the lid. Obviously Zechariah was not implying that God had removed all wickedness from the world. Rather, he had confined and limited it. God was restraining wickedness and keeping it in check so that it would not run free in the world.

The basket was carried away by two angelic beings to the country of Babylonia, or Babylon. Wickedness would be deposited in the land where humanity first rebelled against God, where a rebel named Nimrod ordered his followers to build a tower whose top would reach God. Later, Babylon was the city that had threatened God's land of promise and sacked and burned Jerusalem.

Wickedness, said the angel, would again reside in Babylon. But how? Zechariah had been living in the land of Babylon when it fell to the Medo-Persians. Could Babylon rise again?

Yes. Zechariah's vision shows that the "house" of Babylon will rise again "when it is ready." The time and place have not been right for thousands of years, but when God's prophetic plan is ready, Babylon will be rebuilt. Wickedness will again reign from the plain of Babylon. The city where humanity's rebellion against God began will be the site where that rebellion will return to take up residence.

Every day that passes brings us closer to the end times, and every day the eyes of the world focus more closely on events in the Middle East and Mesopotamia. One key element in God's program of end-time activities will be the reestablishment of Babylon as a world power, when wickedness will again occupy the "city of man."

As Babylon takes its place in the center of the world stage, it is time to open our eyes.

2
A Royal Mandate

When King Nebuchadnezzar ran things around
here some 2,500 years ago, he left clear instructions for the future kings of Babylon that are
finally being carried out. Writing in cuneiform
script on tablets of clay, the royal scribes urged
their master's successors to repair and rebuild
his temples and palaces. Today, in a gesture rich
in political significance, President Saddam Hussein, Iraq's strong-armed ruler, is sparing no
effort to obey that now-distant command.

PAUL LEWIS in the *San Francisco Chronicle*[1]

For nearly two thousand years, Babylon was
the most important city in the world. It was the commercial and financial center for all Mesopotamia, the
center of a geographical "X" that linked the Orient with
the Mediterranean and Egypt with Persia. Its scribes
and priests spread its cultural heritage throughout the
known world. The arts of divination, astronomy, astrology, accounting, and private commercial law all sprang
from Babylon.[2]

Still, Babylon declined in importance as the major
routes of commerce and trade shifted from the shores
of the Euphrates to those of the Tigris. First Seleucia,

then Ctesiphon, and in turn Baghdad rose to become the center of power and influence. Babylon was still inhabited, though the city retained only a shadow of its former glory. It had not yet fallen in the way predicted by the prophets, but its glory had been eclipsed by others.

By the beginning of the twentieth century, as Babylon crumbled into the shifting sands of the desert, it seemed unlikely that it would ever rise from the mounds that had entombed it for so long.

In 1980, all that existed on the site of ancient Babylon were dusty ruins, or ruins of ruins. Babylon's walls, made from clay bricks, were not as strong as the still-imposing stone structures of Egypt. Barely a wall was intact.

But during the next two decades, over sixty million bricks were laid in the reconstruction of Nebuchadnezzar's fabled city. Saddam Hussein ignored the objections of archaeologists who considered it a crime to build over ancient ruins. He scrapped a plan to rebuild Babylon on a nearby site across the Euphrates River. On the exact site of ancient Babylon, he has reconstructed the southern palace of Nebuchadnezzar, including the Procession Street, a Greek theater, many temples, what was once Nebuchadnezzar's throne room, and a half-scale model of the Ishtar Gate.

An artificial hill, almost a hundred feet high, has been built next to Nebuchadnezzar's palace and planted with palm trees and vines. Since the end of the Gulf War, Saddam Hussein has constructed a magnificent palace for himself on this hill. His palace looks down on the one once occupied by King Nebuchadnezzar, perhaps to show that he expects his glory to eclipse that of his predecessor.

Babylon. The name has given me shivers ever since I read about it as a child. But finally visiting it, one white-hot day in Iraq, had a grisly poignancy I hadn't expected to find. . . .
But in the background, on a nearby hillside, is another of Saddam's constructions. It's one of his fabled palaces, his own personal Babylon; a building so large it might easily hold a crowd of 10,000.
RICK MACINNES-RAE for *CBC Radio*[3]

Hussein plans to rebuild the hanging gardens, once considered one of the seven wonders of the world: He offered a $1.5 million prize to the Iraqi engineer who could devise a plan to irrigate the gardens using only the technology available in ancient Babylon. And the ziggurat, or "Tower of Babel," may also once again rear over the city.

In the next few years, [Director General of Antiquities, Dr. Muayad] Said predicts, the government will also redig and refill the city moat, close the city to all traffic but pedestrians and horse-drawn carriages, and maybe rebuild the ziggurat.
AMY SCHWARTZ in the *Washington Post*[4]

The Building Begins

The restoration of Babylon began in 1978 to save what remained of the city from the destructive effects of local salt deposits, a high water table, and pillaging from local villagers. In part because most young Iraqi men were away at the war with Iran, and in part because native laborers often lacked the required skills, the early reconstruction was done through the hands of over eighteen hundred Egyptian, Sudanese, Chinese, and South Korean laborers.

The Iraqis are determined that the new Babylon will look as nearly like the old as possible. No one is exactly sure how the ancient city looked. Scholars, however, are studying archaeological data and other information from ancient Sumerian and Babylonian writings in order to make sure that the restored Babylon is authentic.

The reports of the German archaeologist Robert Koldewey, who excavated much of Babylon between 1899 and 1912, would have moldered away on library shelves except for the strange turn of political events that have thrust his work into prominence today. His black-and-white maps of the ancient city of Babylon have led first to blueprints and then to yellow brick and mortar.

The German archaeologists who excavated the area carried off the best remains of ancient Babylon. The blue glazed bricks of the original Ishtar Gate, decorated with bulls and fanciful dragons, are now in the Pergamon Museum in Berlin. The great black stones of Hammurabi, on which were written one of civilization's first known law codes, now reside in the Louvre in Paris. Hussein's government has petitioned to have the original items returned, but no one realistically expects them to arrive.

Will Tourists Flock to "Babylon World"?

Some observers believe that Babylon is being rebuilt as a tourist attraction and little more. It has been described as "a kind of megalomaniacal Disneyland." Amy Schwartz, an editorial writer for the *Washington Post,* called it "one of the world's oddest attractions . . . with jiggly music, . . . a plethora of snack bars and rest areas and a 'Lake Saddam' for fishing."[5]

The long-range plans for Babylon include hotels, playgrounds, recreation centers, movie theaters, and temples. The main hotel in the tourist city, like the supposed ruins of the Tower of Babel, will resemble a ziggurat, a pyramid-like structure with outside staircases and a shrine at the top.

When I attended the first two Babylonian Festivals in 1987 and 1988, guests from all over the world were gathered. There were ballet troupes from Russia and France, opera singers from Italy, folk dancers from Greece, Turkey, and Poland, flamenco artists from Spain, and Bedouin dancers from Saudi Arabia. The Iraqis even invited Madonna, who didn't show.

"This is not just an Iraqi festival," Munir Bashir told a writer for the *Los Angeles Times.* "It is a festival for the whole world, because Babylon was the capital of civilization once and has given the world so much. People from all over the world want to see Babylon. All the time we have requests."[6]

A Pardon for Babylon?

Iraqis enjoy Nebuchadnezzar's emerging palace, flocking to Babylon by rickety bus and car on their Friday holiday. "It's prettier than where we live," said Sadia, a teenage student who was visiting with friends. Noisy wedding parties drive over, too, each led by trumpeters and drummers who vie to produce the loudest cacophony.[7]

PAUL LEWIS in the *San Francisco Chronicle*

There may be another subtle reason, however, behind the drive to rebuild Babylon. Michael Ross, a writer for the *Los Angeles Times,* speculated that perhaps Munir Bashir took the job of organizing the music for the Babylon Music Festival to "grant Babylon a pardon from the biblical sentence imposed upon it in the book of Revelation, when a 'mighty' angel cast a stone into the sea and said: So shall Babylon the great city be thrown down with violence, and shall be found no more: and the sound of harpists and minstrels, of flute players and trumpeters, shall be heard in thee no more."[8]

But because music and building and wedding celebrations continue in the city of Babylon, we know that it is too soon to grant such a pardon: The violent destruction of the city has not yet occurred. The passage in Revelation 18:22–23 continues:

No workman of any trade will ever be found in you again. The sound of a millstone will never be heard in you again. The light of a lamp will never shine in you again. The voice of bridegroom and bride will never be heard in you again.

Why is Saddam Hussein rebuilding Babylon? Some Iraqis, noticing that the rebuilding began in earnest during the years of war with Iran, see Hussein's building campaign as a living reminder to his people of the feud that has existed between his people and the Persians (who live in present-day Iran) for thousands of years.

The president has signed an open check to reconstruct the ancient city and revive the marvelous shape it had before the Persian aggression which destroyed it more than 20 centuries ago.
BABYLON GOVERNOR ARIF GITA SUHEIL[9]

Others believe Hussein's goal is to reestablish Iraq as the cradle of civilization and the Iraqi people as heirs to the great cultures of Babylon, Nineveh, and Ur, which flourished thousands of years ago between the Tigris and Euphrates Rivers.

It is time to look more closely at Saddam Hussein's reasons for rebuilding.

3
Why Rebuild Babylon?

In the January 16, 1987, issue of the *Los Angeles Times*, Michael Ross wrote: "Babylon has assumed additional importance for the government since the war broke out in September, 1980. Keen on establishing a link between its current conflict with the Persians and the legendary battles of the past, the Iraqi government has speeded up the reconstruction in order to make Babylon a symbol of national pride."[1]

To appreciate the present-day construction of Babylon, it is necessary to understand Iraq's recent history. In February 1963, Iraq was rocked by a bloody coup. The Pan Arab Socialist Renaissance Party, more commonly called the Baath Party, took power. Goals of the Baath Party include the political unification of all Arabs and the glorification of the Arabs as a race. The Baath Party has opposed, and still opposes, Jewish immigration into the land of Israel and the establishment of an independent Jewish state.

Saddam Hussein, a Baathist, became president of Iraq and chairman of the Revolutionary Command Council in July 1979. Since assuming leadership, he has become the driving force to make Iraq a leader among the Arab countries. His name means "one who confronts," and six days after becoming president he confronted twenty-two of his rivals in leadership and had them executed. He was now the sole ruler of Iraq, but he had not yet achieved his ultimate ambition. His goal was—and is—to become nothing less than the savior and leader of the Arab world.

Saddam Hussein thinks in terms of circles. . . . His most immediate circle is the gulf, which remains No. 1 for him. But beyond that there is the circle of the Arab world, where he aspires to hegemony, to being the single most important leader. . . . He sees himself as Nasser's heir in the Arab world.
AMITZIA BARAM, Haifa University[2]

Hussein's First Invasion

In 1980, one year after assuming power, Hussein invaded Iran, hoping to take advantage of the recent change of leadership in Iran and the resulting chaos. Hussein's reasons for invading Iran were complex, but an underlying problem is the racial tensions that have existed between Iraq and Iran for thousands of years. The two countries share the Islamic religion, but Iranians are not Arabs. They are Persians who speak Farsi rather than Arabic and have a distinct social, cultural, and ethnic heritage. Hammurabi of Babylon fought the Persians eighteen hundred years before Christ. In 539 B.C. Cyrus, king of Persia, conquered Babylon.

It is often difficult for the American mind to comprehend, but the people of the Middle East talk of centuries-old feuds as if they began yesterday. The feud between the Iraqis and the Iranians (Persians), who are now at peace, could be energetically kick-started at practically a moment's notice. In that area of the world, any lingering hostility between various ethnic groups can be inflamed into war with one impassioned breath.

A second reason for Iraq's invasion of Iran was political. After the overthrow of the shah of Iran, Khomeini's Islamic Republic tried to topple Iraq's Baathist regime by supporting the Kurdish rebels in northern Iraq and by appealing to the Shiite Muslims in Iraq (the Baath government is dominated by Sunni Muslims). The Kurds, who are not Arabs, want to be free of Arab domination. Hussein invaded Iran, then, to retaliate for Iran's interference in Iraqi affairs.

A third reason for the invasion was geographical. Landlocked Iraq, which is oil rich, has only twenty-six miles of coastline on the Persian Gulf. Basra, Iraq's inland port, lies fifty miles from the Persian Gulf on the Shatt al Arab waterway. This waterway forms the border between Iraq and Iran, and both countries claim control of the waters. Hussein felt his vital access to the gulf was threatened by the Iran-Iraq compromise of 1975, and he was convinced that he could win a secure link to the sea.

War Changes Babylon's Importance

Before the Iran-Iraq War, portions of Babylon had been restored. Some areas were excavated, a museum was built, and one temple was reconstructed. The area, however, was primarily of interest to archaeologists and scholars. Only after the beginning of the war with Iran did the reconstruction of Babylon become a priority.

In 1982, Iraq published a booklet titled *Babylon*. The chief message of the book appears on the back cover: "Archaeological Survival of Babylon is a Patriotic, National, and International Duty." The book was remarkable because it called for international assistance in rebuilding Babylon. Saddam Hussein wanted Babylon rebuilt, but his goal was to rebuild it only as an archaeological park that would focus on the "preservation and restoration of the monuments of Babylon."[3]

But sometime between 1982 and 1987, Hussein's purpose for restoring Babylon changed.

Grim News on the War Front

When Saddam Hussein invaded Iran in 1980, he expected to win a rapid victory over the demoralized Iranian army. The army, which had been loyal to the shah of Iran, had lost power to the religious clerics who now ruled the country. Hussein expected his army, the fourth largest in the world, to crush the Iranians easily. He was wrong.

The war that was going to end in weeks stretched into months and then years. From 1982 to 1988 the tide turned against the Iraqis, who were driven from Iranian territory in fierce, bloody battles. The relentless Iranians continued to send wave after wave of Revolutionary Guard volunteers at the Iraqi positions. The war turned into a stalemate that neither side could break.

News from the front lines was grim, and so was the mood in Baghdad. The early flush of excitement gave way to fear and uncertainty. The city, within range of Iranian missiles, suffered physical damage. More significant was the toll in human suffering and death. During the war's eight years, an estimated one hundred and thirty thousand Iraqis died. Another three hundred thousand were injured. Almost every family in Iraq felt the sting of death. Day after day, bullet-riddled taxis laden with flag-draped coffins brought the bodies of young Iraqi men home to families who had last seen their loved ones walking off to war.

Not only was the war costly in lives; it also drained the Iraqi treasury. Before the war began, oil-rich Iraq had a surplus of $30 billion, but after the war the country owed $70 billion. The tremendous cost of outfitting and deploying an army of one million men was staggering. Worst of all, the price of oil was dropping on world markets, and Iraq's pumping and shipping facilities were being destroyed by Iranian shells and bombs. Iraq's oil production dropped from 4.5 million barrels a day to a mere trickle after the war began.

It all spelled trouble for Saddam Hussein, who survived several assassination attempts. He soon realized he needed some force to galvanize the will of the people, or he would be swept away in a sea of discontent. He needed some way to crystallize his people's ancient enmity for Iran, some symbol of Iraqi superiority. What better way to dramatize the situation than to point to the ruins of Babylon, the city that had been conquered by a Persian king?

President Hussein's decision to rebuild Nebuchadnezzar's Palace at the height of a war he almost lost was the centerpiece of a campaign to strengthen Iraqi nationalism by appealing to history. Mr. Hussein's campaign also served subtler ends; it justified Iraq's costly war with Iran as the continuation of Mesopotamia's ancient feud with Persia. And it portrayed Saddam Hussein as successor to Nebuchadnezzar, Babylon's mightiest ruler.

PAUL LEWIS in the *New York Times International*[4]

Nation Building

History is often used in nation building in that part of the world.

PROFESSOR J. C. HUREWITZ, Columbia University[5]

The city of Babylon was a supreme visual aid. It became an Iraqi Alamo or Masada. Saddam Hussein's decision to rebuild Babylon forced the people to focus on a grand era in Iraq's history, a time when they had been defeated by the same enemy who again threatened the nation.

Building Babylon became synonymous with rising to the Iranian threat and asserting Iraq's "manifest destiny" to lead the Arab nations to glory. Now, instead of just building Babylon as an archaeological park, Hussein made Babylon the focal point of Iraqi nationalism, which had replaced the earlier Baathist goal of Arab nationalism. By early 1987, plans were under way to hold the first annual Babylon Festival to celebrate the glory of Babylon, which included an emphasis on Saddam Hussein and Iraq.

It is no accident that the opening of the festival was scheduled for September 22, 1987—seven years to the day after Iraq's invasion of Iran.[6]

Son of Nebuchadnezzar

It's a Mesopotamian tradition that whenever a new ruler arose, he would rebuild all the principal cities of Mesopotamia.

DR. MUAYAD SAID, Director, General of Antiquities for Iraq[7]

By rebuilding Nebuchadnezzar's city, Hussein has a natural opportunity to portray himself as Nebuchadnezzar's successor. Understandably, the rulers of Syria, Jordan, Israel, and Saudi Arabia are nervous when Hussein extols Nebuchadnezzar's kingdom and leadership, for the ancient king ruled the lands of the entire Arab world.[8]

When I attended the Babylon Festival as an invited

participant, I could not help noticing the emphasis placed on Saddam Hussein and the comparisons between Hussein and Nebuchadnezzar. The festival's official seal featured the two men's portraits side by side, stressing their physical similarities. The festival's official theme was revealing: "From Nabukhadnezzar to Saddam Hussein, Babylon undergoes a renaissance."

On the opening night of the festival, Iraq's Minister of Information and Culture spoke to us. His speech, focusing on the political and historical conflict between Iraq and her enemies, appeared in the newspaper the next day:

The Persian [Iranian] mentality in our neighborhood, prompted by deep-rooted hatred and aggressiveness, tried to quench the flame of civilization in this city of Babylon. Hence the city came under the attack of the Persian ruler Kurash [Cyrus] who, before 2500 years, laid siege to this town. The siege lasted long and the town remained strong. It was not until Cyrus had collaborated with the Jews inside the city that he was able to tighten the siege round the city and subsequently to occupy it. . . . Today we are living in the midst of Khomeini's aggression which has extended over a span of seven years during which Khomeini had allied himself with the Zionists in an attempt to enter Baghdad and other Iraqi cities and destroy them as was the case with Babylon. . . . It [rebuilt Babylon] will serve as a living example of the grandeur of the Iraqis to pursue their path for more glories.

MR. LATIF NSAYYIF JASSIM, Iraqi Minister of Information and Culture[9]

Another Old Enemy Arises

Iran was not the only country to confront Hussein in the early 1980s. On June 7, 1981, Israeli warplanes made a daring raid on the Osirak nuclear reactor near Baghdad, destroying Iraq's fledgling attempt to develop nuclear weapons. The attack humiliated and angered Hussein. Iraq had always opposed the state of Israel, sending troops to fight in each of the Arab-Israeli wars. Now the Israelis had struck close to Baghdad and destroyed a strategic plant Hussein had personally traveled to France to secure.

Iraq's hatred of Israel also played prominently in Hussein's decision to rebuild Babylon. Saddam had always been one of Israel's most recalcitrant enemies, and he knew that one rallying cry to unite the Arab people was *Al-Quds*—Jerusalem! He searched for a common cause around which Arabs could unite, and found it in the "liberation of Palestine" from Israel.

(All, that is, except Egypt. When the Camp David Accords were signed in 1978, Iraq led the other Arab nations in condemning Egypt. At the 1978 Baghdad summit the Arab nations followed Iraq's lead and broke diplomatic ties with Egypt because of the peace treaty with Israel. Those ties were not restored until 1983.)

Again, Babylon and Nebuchadnezzar played a central role in Hussein's plan, this time in uniting the Arabs against Israel. The official program for the 1987 Babylon Festival featured an opening statement from Saddam Hussein to the participants:

Old policies have always ignored the status of
Babylon when they created psychological and sci-
entific barriers between Iraqis and their leaders in
ancient times. No one has ever mentioned the
achievements of "Hammurabi," the founder of the
first organized sets of law in human history. Or
"Nebuchadnezzar," the national hero who was able
to defeat the enemies of the nation on the land of
"Kennan" [Canaan] and to take them as prisoners
of war to Babylon. What we need now is to
increase awareness in this regard.

SADDAM HUSSEIN[10]

Nebuchadnezzar was the only ruler ever able to lead
the armies of Mesopotamia against the Israelites and
defeat them in battle. Nebuchadnezzar took the land of
Judah from the Israelites. By rebuilding Babylon, Saddam
Hussein was making himself the new Nebuchadnezzar,
who also hoped to lead the Arab armies in victory over
Israel.

Colorful murals appear on the outer courtyard walls
of the Nebuchadnezzar Museum in Babylon. One depicts
Nebuchadnezzar supervising the construction of a temple, another shows him looking over the city he has
built, and a third pictures him leading his army in battle against a city.

In each carefully chosen picture, there is a parallel
to Saddam Hussein. Saddam has rebuilt the temple
originally constructed by Nebuchadnezzar. He is rebuilding the city of Babylon. But he has yet to lead his army
in battle against a city. What is remarkable about the city
in the mural is that it is a walled city in a mountainous

region surrounded by a prominent valley—clearly Jerusalem. Saddam Hussein wants to parallel the life of Nebuchadnezzar by leading his army against Israel and Jerusalem!

When Mrs. Jaafar, the archaeologist, was asked if Iraqis considered Mr. Hussein to be "the new Nebuchadnezzar," she laughed and replied, "Yes, of course!" Among Arabs, King Nebuchadnezzar is remembered as much as anything for the fact that he three times conquered Jerusalem, carrying tens of thousands of Jews back to Babylon.

JOHN BURNS in the *New York Times International*[11]

Babylon, then, has become far more than an archaeological project. It is a symbol of Iraqi greatness. It represents the goals and dreams of Iraqis to be the guiding light and dominant force in all Arab countries. The new Babylonian/Iraqi empire aspires to achieve worldwide respect and honor again for the Arab people and to avenge decades of humiliation and defeat at the hands of the Israelis.

Hussein is the leader who has carefully crafted this goal, but he is not alone in this vision. He has articulated the longing of Arabs in general and of the Iraqi people in particular. Babylon and the empire of Nebuchadnezzar conjure up the magic of Arab unity and greatness that has inspired a host of would-be conquerors through the centuries.

Hussein's call for a united Arab uprising against Israel—and against the United States because of our support for Israel—has increased his popularity. Since the Gulf War, Hussein has portrayed himself as the one man who dared oppose the West—and who remained in power in spite of all attempts by the United States to crush him.

At the time of the Gulf War, Yasser Arafat and the PLO publicly sided with Saddam Hussein. And Hussein has not forgotten this strategic ally. During the PLO's two-year campaign of terror against Israel, Hussein paid a $25,000 cash bounty to the families of suicide bombers. That appealed to the Muslim fundamentalists who believe that the "Christian" West has conspired with Israel against Islam.

Amr Moussa, secretary-general of the Arab League, said an American war [against Iraq] would "open the gates of hell" in the Middle East. . . . because Arab governments are convinced that America is so loathed on "the street" that a war might see instability cartwheel throughout the region, shaking pro-U.S. governments in Egypt, Jordan, and Saudi Arabia.[12]

Michael Elliot in *Time*

The coming attack on Iraq will be an attack on the whole Arab region, and will completely reshape its history.

Muhammad Abd al-Fattah Muhsin in *Al-Ahram*[13]

But to understand the present—and the future—we must journey back to the past.

4
Babylon's Rebellious Beginnings

Babylon has been, at different times in history, a shining light showing the best that humankind can offer. During its glory days, it gave the world a law code, magnificent buildings, and the hanging gardens, one of the seven wonders of the world. Babylon boasted many great warriors, and its best-known king, Nebuchadnezzar, easily mowed down nations as he trekked across the region.

Babylon had a proud beginning. The Garden of Eden was located near the Euphrates River, and early civilization spread out from that region. In the days immediately after the Flood, God gave Noah and his children specific instructions for repopulating the earth:

> *"Be fruitful and increase in number and fill the earth. . . . Be fruitful and increase in number; multiply on the earth and increase upon it."*
> GENESIS 9:1, 7

God's command to Noah reminds us of His earlier words to Adam and Eve: "Be fruitful and increase in number; fill the earth and subdue it" (Genesis 1:28). God's gracious protection of Noah and his family in the ark allowed them to become the new Adam and Eve of the post-Flood world. They were given another chance to live according to God's will, to spread out across the entire world and form families that would live in obedience to God.

Unfortunately, humanity's problem is not centered in the environment or in circumstances—our problem is our sinful and rebellious heart. Scarcely had the door of the ark cracked open on Mount Ararat when the next crisis erupted between God and His creation. Genesis 9 goes on to give the sad account of Noah's drunkenness and Ham's inappropriate and disrespectful behavior. The world again began its descent down the slippery slope of rebellion against God.

Nimrod: Babylon's Founding Father

The character flaws evident in Noah's youngest son, Ham, developed and expanded in Ham's children (Genesis 9:22–27). Some of the nations and peoples that developed from Ham's line included Egypt, the Babylonians, the Assyrians, and the various groups of Canaanites. Virtually all of Israel's major enemies in biblical history came from the line of Ham.

Genesis 10 lists Ham's descendants, and tucked in the midst of this list of names is Nimrod.

> *Cush was the father of Nimrod, who grew to be a mighty warrior on the earth. He was a mighty hunter before the* LORD. *. . . . The first centers of his kingdom were Babylon. . . ."*
> GENESIS 10:8–10

The name *Nimrod* could come from the Babylonian name *Namra-uddu,* a form of the name for Marduk, Babylon's chief god. Or it could come from the Babylonian name *Nu-marad,* "man of Marad."[1] Moses most likely used a play on words by spelling Nimrod's name in the Genesis account so that it sounded like the Hebrew word for "rebel" *(marad).* Nimrod was a rebel, and the cities he founded were rebellious cities.

Moses described Nimrod as a "mighty warrior" and a "mighty hunter before the LORD." Kings of that time traditionally demonstrated their right to rule people by displaying prowess over the animal kingdom. Just as professional athletes are admired and respected today, Nimrod's hunting skills and physical abilities added to his standing in society and rocketed him into a position of leadership.

Nimrod's mighty skills were known in a special way to God. I believe H. L. Ellison captured the idea when he wrote that Nimrod "showed his right to rule over the kingdom he had created by force by killing the animal creation that God had entrusted to him."[2] Nimrod directed his God-given skills and natural abilities toward conquest and subjugation. And this was the beginning of Babylon.

Babel: Man's Tower of Trouble

Babylon was a city conceived in rebellion. Nimrod was the architect of man's union against God, and Genesis 11:1–9 records the catastrophic consequences of his actions. God commanded Noah and his children to "fill the earth" following their departure from the ark. But what God intended for good, the people perceived as a threat. They were afraid to separate, afraid to go to new lands, afraid to rely on God's strength instead of their own.

Though Nimrod's name is not used in Genesis 11, chapter 10 informs us that he was the chief leader in the movement to build a center at Babylon. Moses describes the initial settlement on "a plain in Shinar," the broad plain of the Tigris and Euphrates Rivers south of present-day Baghdad.

The area is a somewhat flat alluvial plain. The Tigris and Euphrates Rivers meander through on their way to the Persian Gulf, supplying water for drinking and irrigation to a land that would otherwise be bare desert. Those two rivers provide life, and by using canals and irrigation, civilizations have flourished in the Mesopotamian region for centuries.

There are no mountains on the plain of Shinar and,

consequently, no stones for building materials. But what the land lacks in rock, it offers in oil. The oil that today powers much of the world was also used in the days of Nimrod.

> They said to each other, "Come, let's make bricks and bake them thoroughly." They used brick instead of stone, and tar for mortar. Then they said, "Come, let us build ourselves a city, with a tower that reaches to the heavens, so that we may make a name for ourselves and not be scattered over the face of the whole earth."
>
> GENESIS 11:3–4

Because the people lacked stones with which to build, they baked bricks. In place of crushed limestone, they used tar as mortar. William White, describing the city archaeologically, noted that "brick and mud-wall construction occurred everywhere."[3]

People still use brick for building in that region, and often the bricks are dried in the sun. But for permanent construction, the people use kiln-fired bricks for added strength. The builders of Babel used kiln-fired bricks because they wanted their project to last.

The focus of their efforts was to be a city with a tower, or ziggurat, that reached to the heavens. The purpose for the tower at Babylon, as well as that of the later ziggurats, was to serve as a "staircase" from earth to heaven. Human beings wanted to reach God by their own efforts.

Moses describes the tower as "a tower that reaches to the heavens" (Genesis 11:4). This may have been the actual name of the tower as well as an accurate description. The ziggurat at Babylon later rebuilt by Nebuchadnezzar was named *Etemenanki* ("the building which is the foundation of heaven and earth").[4]

For Man's Glory and Honor

The people wanted to make a name for themselves. Having rejected God's expressed will, these descendants of Noah decided to construct a monument to their own greatness and glory. They didn't realize that a truly great name comes only from God, and that the Nimrods of this world are easily superseded by men like Abraham, to whom God said, "I will make your name great" (Genesis 12:2).

The people began to build. They gathered in the first city recorded in the Bible, under a rebel leader, to work together for their own glory and honor. Then, Moses writes, God "came down" (verse 5) to view this tower which man intended to reach "to the heavens." No matter how high they built, God was still far out of reach.

God's concern was not that their building was too tall, but rather that humankind had united in opposition to Him. "If as one people speaking the same language they have begun to do this, then nothing they plan to do will be impossible for them" (Genesis 11:6). Obviously God did not have to worry that humanity would become too much for Him to handle. His power and majesty far surpass anything these people possessed.

Gerhard von Rad gives a logical explanation of God's concern: "God's eye already sees the end of the road upon which mankind has entered with this deed, the possibilities and temptations which such a massing of forces holds. . . . Therefore God resolves upon a punitive, but at the same time preventive, act, so that he will not have to punish man more severely as his degeneration surely progresses."[5]

The union of Nimrod and his followers embraced all mankind to the exclusion of God. Had their plan succeeded, the world would have been again as it was before the Flood when "every inclination of the thoughts of [man's] heart was only evil all the time" (Genesis 6:5).

Therefore God "confused the language of the whole world" (Genesis 11:9). He unraveled the fabric of the society humanity was trying to weave. The builders tried to build a gateway to God, but God turned their effort into confusion.

Before the confusion at Babel, the world had one language and a common speech. But after God's judgment, people scattered throughout the world, failures at their attempt to "make a name for themselves," victims of the very fate they had feared and tried to avoid. Their plan was supplanted by God's plan for human redemption through the seed of Abraham, the man whose name God chose to make great.

Babel was humanity's first united attempt to short-circuit God's purpose. This first post-Flood city was designed expressly to thwart God's plan for humankind. The people wanted unity and power, and Babel was to be the seat of that power. Babylon, the city of man trying to rise to heaven, was built in direct opposition to God's plan.

Then they said, "Come, let us build ourselves a city, with a tower that reaches to the heavens."

GENESIS 11:4

I saw the Holy City, the new Jerusalem, coming down out of heaven from God, prepared as a bride beautifully dressed for her husband.

REVELATION 21:2

Quite a contrast, isn't it?

5
A Tale of Two Cities

It was the best of times, it was the worst of times, it was the age of wisdom, it was the age of foolishness, it was the epoch of belief, it was the epoch of incredulity, it was the season of Light, it was the season of Darkness, it was the spring of hope, it was the winter of despair, we had everything before us, we had nothing before us, we were all going direct to Heaven, we were all going direct the other way. . . .

CHARLES DICKENS, *A Tale of Two Cities*[1]

Dickens wrote that immortal paragraph to describe the worlds of two cities, London and Paris, at the time of the French Revolution. But his words describe very well the situation of two contemporary and future cities, Jerusalem and Babylon. In the conflict between God and Satan, good and evil, righteousness and rebellion, Jerusalem and Babylon are like opposite poles of a magnet.

Jerusalem represents the positive pole of God's plan for His creation. It is the city selected by God as His dwelling place, the capital of God's kingdom on earth, the city where God's Son died for the sins of the world.

Babylon represents the negative pole of humanity's attempts to usurp God's authority. It is the city of rebellion where humanity reared up its tower in defiance of God, the city that eventually destroyed Jerusalem and started the "Time of the Gentiles."

And yet, like the poles of a magnet, these two cities have been drawn together throughout history. It is impossible to fully understand the history of one city without understanding its relationship to the other.

The City of God and the City of Man

The conflict between these two cities has often been spiritualized. Augustine, for example, spiritualized the conflict between these two forces as he described the "City of God" and the "City of Man."[2] But the tale of two cities told in the Bible focuses on physical, brick-and-mortar entities, not symbolic ideals. The Babylon described in Revelation is not merely an idea, a religion, or an economic system. It is, above all, a physical city.

The city of man is built on the principle of independence from God. By building the Tower of Babel, human beings first tried to reach heaven on their own, without God's help. But their construction of the "tower that reaches to the heavens" came to a halt when God confounded their language and forced them to scatter throughout the earth. Yet Babylon would return, again and again, for the human heart is constantly seeking its own glory. Only in the last days would it be thrown down forever.

The city of God, by contrast, is built on the principle of dependence upon God and obedience to His will. In Genesis 14 Moses introduces Jerusalem ("Salem") as part of Abram's story. Abram (later renamed Abraham) obeyed God, and God promised to make his name great. Jerusalem would flourish as long as Abraham's descendants would give glory to God. Although it would fall and rise up again, in the last days it would be established as God's city forever.

A Time of Testing

Abram heeded God's call and moved his family to the land God showed him, Canaan. It was a Land of Promise, but it was also a land of testing.[3] Abram struggled to trust God in the face of famine, family strife, and foreign invasion.

Genesis 14 describes an attack by an alliance of four kings from the East against five kings residing in the Land of Promise. It was the initial Gentile threat against God's Promised Land, and God gave Abram victory over the invaders. For the first time we read about Salem, which, under its later name of Jerusalem, became the city chosen by God as His dwelling place among His people.

The four kings who attacked Abram's land were Amraphel, king of Shinar (Babylon); Arioch, king of Ellasar (an ancient city about ten miles north of Ur); Kedorlaomer, king of Elam (Persia, or modern Iran); and Tidal, king of Goiim (who probably ruled over a group of tribes). All four of these attacking kings were from the region of southern Mesopotamia.

These four kings of the East marched against and defeated five kings of the plain located south of the Dead Sea. There must have been some in Abram's camp who wondered if moving to the land of Canaan had been such a good idea! How could a land be called "promised" if invading foreign kings could defeat every king and city standing in their way?

But God had given Abram a promise:

> *"I will make you into a great nation and I will bless you; I will make your name great, and you will be a blessing. I will bless those who bless you, and whoever curses you I will curse; and all peoples on earth will be blessed through you."*
> GENESIS 12:2–3

Here was the first great test of God's promise and Abram's faith. The situation looked hopeless, but when the four kings left to carry the spoils of conquest back to Mesopotamia, Abram, trusting in God's promise, pursued and defeated them. Melchizedek, king of Salem, proclaimed the source of Abram's victory:

Blessed be God Most High, who delivered your enemies into your hand.

MELCHIZEDEK, King of Salem, (Genesis 14:20)

This is the attitude that characterizes the city of God.

Invaders from Shinar

It is interesting that the biblical account of this invasion places a great deal of emphasis on Amraphel, king of Shinar. He heads the list of threatening kings, implying that he was the dominant king in the group. Babylon, however, was not the greatest city in the Mesopotamian region at that time. Elam was the strongest and most dominant. In two separate places (Genesis 14:5, 17), Kedorlaomer, king of Elam, is identified as the leader of the allied invaders.

Why, then, does Moses list Amraphel first in Genesis 14:1? I believe it is not a mere coincidence. Moses places Amraphel first because he was from Shinar, or Babylon, the land where humanity first united to oppose God's plans. Once again, men from Shinar had united to oppose God's purpose for the land of Israel.

God had scattered the human race at the Tower of Babel by confounding their language and forcing people into distinct ethnic groups. In Genesis 14, we see a replay of the ancient story. Different social and ethnic groups are trying to unite to threaten the land God has promised to Abram and his seed. Again, leading the rebels, is the city of Shinar—Babylon!

After describing the battles in Genesis 14, Moses describes Abram's meetings with the wicked king of Sodom and the righteous king of Salem. From the righteous king of Salem, Abram receives both bread and a blessing. However, Abram refuses to accept anything from the wicked king of Sodom. The king-priest of Salem invokes the name of "God Most High, Creator of heaven and earth" to bless Abram (verse 19), and Abram invokes the name of "God Most High, Creator of heaven and earth" to refuse anything from the king of Sodom (verse 22).

The Establishment of God's City

Who was Melchizedek, king of Salem? Several clues show us that he was the king of the city later called Jerusalem. First, the name "Salem" comes from the Hebrew word *shalom,* or peace. Salem is synonymous with Zion, where God's dwelling place, the temple, is located.

> *In Judah God is known; his name is great in Israel. His tent is in Salem, his dwelling place in Zion.*
> PSALM 76:1–2

The second reason for identifying Salem with the city of Jerusalem is the specific geographical site associated with both cities. When Abram came to Salem, he met with Melchizedek in the Valley of Shaveh (Genesis 14:17), or the King's Valley. Elsewhere the King's Valley is identified as the valley near Jerusalem where Absalom erected a pillar or monument to himself (2 Samuel 18:18). Some believe the valley is the Kidron Valley just to the east of Jerusalem.

The third reason for identifying Salem with Jerusalem is the similarity in names for the kings of each city. The name "Melchizedek" comes from two Hebrew words, *"melech"* (king) and *"zedek"* (righteousness). The name could be translated "my king is righteousness" or "the king of righteousness."

Five hundred years later in the book of Joshua we are introduced to the king of Jerusalem, Adoni-Zedek (Joshua 10:1). In English the names "Melchizedek" and "Adoni-Zedek" do not seem at all alike, but in Hebrew they are very similar. Adoni-Zedek's name could be translated "my lord is righteousness." With only a slight variation, it is still the throne name given to the king of Jerusalem.

A Picture of Blessings to Come

Who was Melchizedek? He was the actual king of Jerusalem who came to bless Abram after his defeat of the four invading kings of the East. But Melchizedek is also used to paint a picture of the final King-Priest of Jerusalem who will rule in righteousness—Jesus Christ. Psalm 110, a psalm about the Messiah, pictures the coming Messiah as both a victorious King and as "a priest forever, in the order of Melchizedek" (verse 4). The writer of Hebrews draws on the imagery of Psalm 110 to show that Melchizedek was a true symbol of Christ as the eternal High Priest.[4] Though Abram spent his life "looking forward to the city with foundations, whose architect and builder is God" (Hebrews 11:10), he caught a glimpse of that great city when he met with Melchizedek.

This chapter of God's "tale of two cities," then, begins with the story of the unholy alliance of kings from the East who marched upon Abram and his people in the land promised to them. Shinar, where the human race first organized in rebellion against God, led the list of nations opposing God's plans for Abram. The threat to God's promised blessing again originated in Babylon.

Babylon and Jerusalem—one is a city of rebellion and warfare, the other a city of peace. One tries to attack, plunder, and despoil the Land of Promise, the other fellowships with the man of promise. One is defeated by Abram, the other is paid tithes by Abram. One is the city of man; the other is the City of God.

6
Judah's Foreign Policy Nightmare

After Abram's defeat of Amraphel and his allies, Babylon stepped off the stage of biblical history for over thirteen hundred years. The Bible does not record Babylon's history, because it did not bear on the history of Israel. The biblical account of history focuses tightly on Abram—now called Abraham—his family, and the nation of Israel. Yet Babylon was busy earning its place in the history books.

From 1900 to 1600 B.C., Babylon entered its first period of international importance with the first Babylonian dynasty. The golden age of this period was the reign of Hammurabi, who codified the laws of Babylon and extended the empire. During his reign, 1792–1750 B.C., the nation of Israel was living in Egypt.

The biblical curtain does not rise again on Babylon until the time of Israel's divided monarchy. The northern kingdom, Israel, had been captured and carried off by the Assyrians. Only the southern kingdom, Judah, remained as the home for God's people. The relationship of Judah to Babylon was very complex. The story is not neatly contained in only the historical books of the Bible. Instead, it can also be found scattered throughout the pages of Isaiah, Jeremiah, Ezekiel, and Daniel.

The influence of Babylon is woven throughout the biblical narrative.
GERALD LARUE[1]

Babylon did not come into contact with Abraham's descendants in any significant way until the time of King Hezekiah. But from the time of Hezekiah until the time of the Babylonian captivity, an observable relationship between Jerusalem and Babylon can be established. For a time, there was an *age of cooperation* as the two countries united against a common enemy. There followed an *age of confrontation* as the two nations squared off against each other in a battle for national autonomy.

The Age of Cooperation

From 715 B.C. until 601 B.C. there was no hostility between Judah and Babylon. In fact, on several occasions the two nations acted in harmony against Assyria, the dominant power in the Middle East at that time. Many countries, including Babylon and Judah, contested Assyria's domination and attempted to cast off its yoke of bondage. While Babylon constantly troubled Assyria's eastern boundaries, Egypt continually stirred up trouble in the west.

Assyria was a cruel nation whose kings used harsh means to acquire and maintain its empire. "In general the Assyrian empire was a huge military machine, existing by means of and for the sake of war, possibly because the Assyrians felt threatened and saw no other way to govern than by force. . . . The kings boasted of the way they mutilated, flayed, impaled, and roasted their captives."[2]

History has often shown that the best way to join two hostile countries is to pit them against a common enemy. The hungry war machine of Assyria forged a spirit of cooperation between Hezekiah, king of Judah, and Merodach-Baladan, son of Baladan, king of Babylon.

A Get-Well Visit

At that time Merodach-Baladan son of Baladan king of Babylon sent Hezekiah letters and a gift, because he had heard of Hezekiah's illness. Hezekiah received the messengers and showed them all that was in his storehouses—the silver, the gold, the spices and the fine oil—his armory and everything found among his treasures. There was nothing in his palace or in all his kingdom that Hezekiah did not show them.

2 KINGS 20:12–13[3]

Merodach-Baladan was a tribal chief from southern Babylon who seized Babylon's throne in 721 B.C. in the confusion following the death of Shalmaneser V, the king of Assyria. Merodach-Baladan reigned from 721 to 710 B.C. and for a short period in 704–703 B.C. When he was not on the throne, he was either plotting his return to power or doing battle with the Assyrians.

Merodach-Baladan came to visit Hezekiah, king of Judah, on the pretext of asking about his health. Hezekiah had faced two calamities in the recent past: He had been seriously ill, and he had been attacked by Sennacherib, king of Assyria.

Sennacherib had led his army in 703 B.C. against Babylon and Merodach-Baladan. The Assyrian king captured the city, and Merodach-Baladan fled with his life.

In my first campaign I accomplished the defeat of Merodach-Baladan, king of Babylonia, together with the army of Elam, his ally, in the plain of Kish. In the midst of that battle he forsook his camp, and made his escape alone; he saved his life. The chariots, horses, wagons, mules, which he left behind at the onset of battle, my hands seized. Into his palace, which is Babylon, joyfully I entered.

SENNACHERIB, King of Assyria[4]

Sennacherib then marched west, systematically moving through Judah and destroying anyone who dared oppose him. His army subdued the rebellious Philistine cities, defeated an Egyptian army that had been sent to aid the rebels, and captured several major

Judean cities in the foothills. He boasted of his accomplishments against Israel.

> But as for Hezekiah, the Jew, who did not bow in submission to my yoke, forty-six of his strong walled towns and innumerable smaller villages in their neighborhood I besieged and conquered by stamping down earth-ramps and then by bringing up battering rams, by the assault of foot soldiers, by breaches, tunneling and sapper operations, I made to come out from them 200,150 people, young and old, male and female, innumerable horses, mules, donkeys, camels, large and small cattle, and counted them as the spoils of war. He himself I shut up like a caged bird within Jerusalem, his royal city.
>
> **SENNACHERIB**[5]

Hezekiah must have been sick in heart as well as in body. News of the capture of other Judean cities reached his ears, and no doubt the king felt powerless. He was gravely ill, shut up in his walled city, his allies defeated. All he could do was pray.

God answered those prayers. During Hezekiah's illness, God sent the prophet Isaiah to give the king good news. God told Isaiah to say, "I will add fifteen years to your life. And I will deliver you and this city from the hand of the king of Assyria" (2 Kings 20:6).

To verify His promise, God gave Hezekiah a sign and reversed the sun's shadow so that it traveled back up ten steps it had gone down on the stairway of Ahaz.[6]

The Assyrian Defeat

Sennacherib attacked Judah, but he stopped short of capturing Jerusalem and killing Hezekiah. In his previous conflicts he had defeated and entered the cities of Babylon, Sidon, Ashdod, Beth-Ammon, Ashkelon, Beth-Dagon, Joppa, Banai-barqa, Azuru, Ekron, Eltekah, and Timnah—but Jerusalem escaped.

God provided deliverance by intervening and killing a hundred and eighty-five thousand Assyrian soldiers (2 Kings 19:34–36). In the midst of a time of uncertainty and upheaval, God restored Hezekiah's health and dealt Sennacherib an unparalleled defeat. So it was a healthy and victorious Hezekiah who gave the envoys from Babylon the grand tour of Jerusalem. It is no surprise that Merodach-Baladan sent emissaries to Jerusalem. Though they asked about Hezekiah's health, they also took care to inquire about his wealth and weaponry. No doubt their purpose was to see if another alliance could be formed against Assyria. Merodach-Baladan was looking for someone to help him regain his throne, and the city of Jerusalem was the only city that had dealt Sennacherib a major blow.

Merodach-Baladan's emissaries also asked Hezekiah about the "miraculous sign that had occurred in the land" (2 Chronicles 32:31). The Babylonians put great faith in astrology and had noticed the strange and sudden shift in the sun, which had been followed by Hezekiah's recovery and the Assyrian army's defeat.

This was Hezekiah's opportunity to share with Merodach-Baladan's envoys the truth about the God of

Israel who controls the planets and stars and delivers kings and nations. Instead, Hezekiah basked in the glory granted to him by the delegation. By showing them his storehouses and armories, he took credit himself for the recent victory over the Assyrians. Hezekiah introduced the Babylonians to Judah's possessions instead of God's power.

Hezekiah's foolish exaltation of himself brought divine judgment. God again sent Isaiah to Hezekiah with an announcement: "The time will surely come when everything in your palace, and all that your fathers have stored up until this day, will be carried off to Babylon" (2 Kings 20:17).

The fulfillment of Isaiah's prediction was over a century away, but the results of Hezekiah's foolishness were inevitable. God had delivered Judah from the Assyrians, but the Assyrians would ultimately fall to the Babylonians. Hezekiah's ally would then become Judah's enemy.

Again Babylon became a stumbling block to God's people. The kingdom of Judah represented God's rule on earth. Though Assyria appeared to be the gravest threat to God's kingdom, it would not be the nation that would ultimately destroy Judah. Instead, Babylon emerged as the true threat to the people of God.

Manasseh

After the time of Hezekiah and Merodach-Baladan, the curtain is drawn on Babylon's relations with Judah for approximately fifty years. During this time Assyria remained the dominant power; however, the fierce nation constantly had to ruthlessly put down challenges to its control. One such challenge brought disaster to the rule of Manasseh, king of Judah.

King Esarhaddon of Assyria rebuilt the city of Babylon that had been destroyed by his father, Sennacherib. He then named his son Ashurbanipal crown prince of Assyria, while making his other son, Shamash-shum-ukin, crown prince of Babylon.

It was not an ideal way to balance power. Eventually, war broke out between the rival brothers. Shamash-shum-ukin, supported by the Elamites, the Chaldean tribes, and other vassal nations, waged war against Ashurbanipal.

After two years, Ashurbanipal gained the upper hand and laid siege to the city of Babylon. By 648 B.C. the city was on the brink of collapse from starvation. Shamash-shum-ukin committed suicide in the flames that consumed his palace. Ashurbanipal then attacked the nations that had allied themselves with Babylon.

How does this history relate to Judah? It is very possible that Manasseh followed the foreign policy of his father Hezekiah and allied himself with Shamash-shum-ukin against Ashurbanipal. If so, this alliance nearly cost Manasseh his life.

The LORD spoke to Manasseh and his people, but they paid no attention. So the LORD brought against them the army commanders of the king of Assyria, who took Manasseh prisoner, put a hook in his nose, bound him with bronze shackles and took him to Babylon.

2 CHRONICLES 33:10–11

The king of Assyria pronounced Manasseh guilty and took him to Babylon for the execution of his sentence. In chains, with a hook through his nose, he was led across the desert and through a noisy, jeering crowd along Babylon's Procession Street. The king of Judah had become a Babylonian trophy, one of the spoils of war.

"In his distress," the biblical account reveals, "he sought the favor of the LORD his God and humbled himself greatly before the God of his fathers. And when he prayed to him, the LORD was moved by his entreaty and listened to his plea; so he brought him back to Jerusalem and to his kingdom. Then Manasseh knew that the LORD is God" (2 Chronicles 33:12–13).

By God's grace, Manasseh was spared and allowed to return to Jerusalem as king. But the city of man was not finished with the City of God.

7
Tainted By Babylon

The kingdom of Assyria dominated Judah from the time of Hezekiah until the time of Josiah. But toward the end of this period a new force began to rise in the east—the Neo-Babylonian Empire. This empire soon surpassed Assyria as the dominant power in the Middle East.

A new king arose in Babylon, Nabopolassar. Through a series of strategic battles he and his son, Nebuchadnezzar, pushed back the Assyrians westward and northward. In 612 B.C., a combined force of Babylonians, Medes, and Scythians attacked and destroyed the Assyrian capital of Nineveh. The Assyrian king, Sin-sharishkun, died in the battle for Nineveh and was replaced by Ashur-uballit II. The Assyrians retreated to Haran but were forced to evacuate because of the unstoppable advance of the Babylonian armies.

Egypt, formerly a foe of the Assyrians, had a curious change in foreign policy and began to support its old enemy. No doubt Egypt recognized the threat posed by Babylon and hoped to prop up the faltering Assyrian state to act as a buffer against this new and unpredictable power.

One of the most crucial battles in this international struggle occurred in 609 B.C. That was the year the remnant of the Assyrian army, with Egyptian support, decided to launch a final counteroffensive against the Babylonian garrison left in Haran. Their objective was to dislodge the Babylonians from the western Euphrates area.

King Josiah of Judah

At that point the Egyptian armies marched onto the pages of biblical history. "While Josiah was king, Pharaoh Neco king of Egypt went up to the Euphrates River to help the king of Assyria. King Josiah marched out to meet him in battle, but Neco faced him and killed him at Megiddo" (2 Kings 23:29).

It appears from the various accounts of this conflict that Josiah understood the purpose of Pharaoh Neco's drive to Carchemish. Why then did he try to hinder the Egyptians in their battle against the Babylonians?

Josiah may have had two reasons for risking his life

in battle. First, he acted from a sense of nationalism. Judah had gained independence from Assyria under Josiah's reign, and Egypt's attempt to support Assyria posed a double threat to Judah's security. Judah could have been threatened by a revived Assyria attempting to regain lost territory, or the nation could have been threatened by an imperialistic Egypt trying to exert influence to the east and north.[1]

Second, Josiah may have acted as an ally in support of Babylon.

> *Neco sent messengers to him [Josiah] saying, "What quarrel is there between you and me, O king of Judah? It is not you I am attacking at this time, but the house with which I am at war."*
>
> 2 CHRONICLES 35:21

Josiah realized that Neco was not interested in encroaching upon the kingdom of Judah. Indications are that Neco fully intended to bypass Judah and had nearly done so. Josiah had not opposed earlier Egyptian expeditions through the land of Israel that had brought reinforcements to the Assyrians.[2] If Josiah had only been interested in protecting his country from Egyptian influence, he would have acted sooner. But Josiah knew that Neco was racing to block the advance of the Babylonian army, and Babylon was an ally of Judah.

It is likely that Josiah had both motives in mind when he decided to oppose the Egyptian advance to Carchemish. There is evidence to suggest that he acted on behalf of the Babylonians, but he also viewed the immediate threat to Judah to be her neighbors on her northern and southern borders—Assyria and Egypt. Babylon was not yet a threat. His fears were justified, for three months after his untimely death at the hands of Pharaoh Neco, the Egyptians intervened in Judah's affairs to appoint a vassal king (2 Chronicles 36:2–4). Thus Judah became a vassal of Egypt—a puppet nation forced to support Egyptian interests.

Whatever his reasons, Josiah supported Babylon. His grandfather, Manasseh, had supported Babylon against Assyria, and his great-grandfather, Hezekiah, had joined with Babylon in trying to throw off Assyria's yoke of bondage. Unfortunately, all three kings found that supporting Babylon ultimately led to national disaster.

The Age of Cooperation Ends

Pharaoh Neco returned from Carchemish with the Egyptian army and seized the kingdom of Judah. King Jehoahaz, after a reign of only three months, was taken in chains to Egypt. His brother, Jehoiakim, was placed on the throne as a loyal vassal of Egypt. The age of Judah's cooperation with Babylon was finished.

Jehoiakim was a political chameleon, and his ever-changing loyalties spelled trouble for Judah. Even as Jehoiakim began to reign, the young prophet Jeremiah started publicly espousing a new message in Jerusalem. Though he still offered the people of Judah opportunity to repent, he began to preach a message of destruction (Jeremiah 26:1–3).

"I will make this house like Shiloh and this city an object of cursing among all the nations of the earth."

JEREMIAH 26:6

The unpopular message nearly cost Jeremiah his life, because the people of Judah felt reasonably secure under Egypt's protection. Still, Jeremiah lifted his prophetic eyes of faith to catch a glimpse of the "foe from the north" God was raising up to judge Judah. That enemy was Babylon.

Jehoiakim served the king of Egypt from 609 to 605 B.C., but then the international balance of power shifted. For four years the Egyptians and Babylonians had faced each other at Carchemish with neither side able to gain the upper hand, but in 605, Nebuchadnezzar scored a decisive victory.

In the twenty-first year the king of Akkad [Nabopolassar, king of Babylon] stayed in his own land. Nebuchadnezzar his eldest son, the crown prince, mustered [the Babylonian army] and took command of his troops; he marched to Carchemish which is on the bank of the Euphrates, and crossed the river [to go] against the Egyptian army which lay in Carchemish. . . . [They] fought with each other and the Egyptian army withdrew before him. He accomplished their defeat and to non-existence [beat?] them. As for the rest of the Egyptian army which had escaped from the defeat [so quickly that] no weapon had reached them, in the district of Hamath the Babylonian troops overtook and defeated them so that not a single man [escaped] to his own country. At that time Nebuchadnezzar

conquered the whole area of the Hatti-country.
THE BABYLONIAN CHRONICLE[3]

Jehoiakim recognized Nebuchadnezzar's superiority and switched allegiance as the Babylonian monarch marched triumphantly through Judah. As the writer of 2 Kings records, "During Jehoiakim's reign, Nebuchadnezzar king of Babylon invaded the land" (2 Kings 24:1).

Normally, Nebuchadnezzar would have secured his control over Judah by deposing its current king and replacing him with someone of his own choosing. But Nebuchadnezzar allowed Jehoiakim to remain on Judah's throne.

There are three reasons why Nebuchadnezzar left Jehoiakim on the throne. First, word reached him that his own father, Nabopolassar, had died on August 15, 605 B.C. Nebuchadnezzar returned home to ascend the throne on September 7, and he may have felt pressure to make a quick return to Babylon to avoid political instability.

Second, Nebuchadnezzar felt that he could gain Jehoiakim's loyalty by taking some "royal hostages" back to Babylon with him. He took with him "some of the Israelites from the royal family," including the prophet Daniel (Daniel 1:3–6).

Finally, Nebuchadnezzar may have considered Judah's history. Jehoiakim's ancestors, Hezekiah and Manasseh, had allied themselves with Babylon; and his father, King Josiah, had even given his life to stop the Egyptians from marching on Babylon. Jehoiakim's brother, Jehoahaz, had been deposed and carried into Egypt as a prisoner. What reason did Nebuchadnezzar have for doubting Jehoiakim's loyalty?

After securing his throne, Nebuchadnezzar returned to the lands he had just captured and consolidated his conquests until early February in 604 B.C. when he gathered his tribute together and returned home to Babylon. With him he took not only "royal hostages," but treasures from God's temple. These he put in the treasure room of his god (Daniel 1:2).

The Chameleon Changes His Colors

Jehoiakim became his [Nebuchadnezzar's] vassal for three years. But then he changed his mind and rebelled against Nebuchadnezzar.

2 KINGS 24:1

Why did Jehoiakim rebel against Babylon? The answer is, again, Egypt. In 601 B.C., Nebuchadnezzar made another advance through the land of Israel. His objective was Egypt, but his army met the Egyptians somewhere in Sinai.

In the fourth year the king of Akkad [Nebuchadnezzar] mustered his army and marched to the Hatti-land [Palestine]. In the month of Kislev [November/December 601 B.C.] he took the lead of his army and marched to Egypt. The king of Egypt heard and mustered his army. In open battle they smote the breast [of] each other and inflicted great havoc on each other. The king of Akkad and his troops turned back and returned to Babylon. In the fifth year the king of Akkad [stayed] in his own land and gathered together his chariots and horses in great numbers.

THE BABYLONIAN CHRONICLE[4]

It seems obvious from this official description of the battle that Nebuchadnezzar's army suffered a serious defeat. The entire next year Nebuchadnezzar was forced to remain in Babylon to repair and equip his battered forces. Jehoiakim saw this as his opportunity to rebel against Babylon and align himself with Egypt. The age of cooperation was over, and the age of confrontation began in earnest.

8
The Age of Confrontation

The prophecy of Isaiah to King Hezekiah now found its fulfillment: Judah fell to Babylon. The period of confrontation with Babylon began in 601 B.C. and lasted until Jerusalem was destroyed in 586.

Although Jehoiakim was free from Babylonian domination for about two years, he was not without difficulty. While reoutfitting his army, Nebuchadnezzar ordered several of his vassal states to launch preliminary strikes against Judah: "The LORD sent Babylonian, Aramean, Moabite, and Ammonite raiders against him . . . to destroy Judah" (2 Kings 24:2).

By mid-December, 598 B.C., Nebuchadnezzar's army was prepared to march against Judah. Nebuchadnezzar's chief objective was to attack Jerusalem and to teach it (and, no doubt, other nations) the awful consequences of rebelling against Babylon. After marching to Judah, he "encamped against the city of Judah and on the second day of the month of Adar he seized the city and captured the king."[1] On March 16, 597 B.C., Jerusalem willingly surrendered.

Ironically, Jehoiakim was dead when Nebuchadnezzar arrived. His son, Jehoiachin, who had reigned for only three months, surrendered to the Babylonians. It is possible that Jehoiakim was assassinated when it became clear that Nebuchadnezzar was coming to attack Jerusalem because of Jehoiakim's defection.[2] The biblical account indicates that Jehoiakim was not a popular ruler (Jeremiah 22:18–19), and it is easy to see how the people might be willing to sacrifice him, hoping to appease Nebuchadnezzar's anger.

Nebuchadnezzar replaced King Jehoiachin, looted the city, and removed its leaders. Yet he still allowed the country to maintain some measure of independence. This implies that those who had initiated the rebellion had been eliminated before his arrival.

The confrontation Judah had dreaded was over— for the moment. Zedekiah was installed as king, and Judah went obediently into the Babylonian camp. In spite of the prophet Jeremiah's warnings, false prophets were predicting a quick end to the Babylonian domination and were urging further insurrection. The land of Judah was a powder keg waiting for a match.

Zedekiah

What Judah needed was a strong leader who would follow the commands of the Lord. Unfortunately, Zedekiah did not qualify. His weakness and vacillation are clearly shown in Jeremiah 38:5, where Zedekiah turns Jeremiah over to government officials with this lame excuse: "He is in your hands. . . . The king can do nothing to oppose you."

The fourth year of Zedekiah's rule was rocked with turmoil. A major insurrection took place in Babylon itself, and no doubt word of this revolt filtered out into the provinces. Jewish nationals eagerly spread rumors and "prophecies" of the soon demise of Nebuchadnezzar and Babylon.[3]

There were stirrings to the south of Judah too. After his defeat at Carchemish, Neco had been fairly ineffective as a deterrent to Babylonian power, except for his victory in 601. When Nebuchadnezzar attacked Jerusalem in 598, the Egyptians stayed home. But in 594 B.C., the coronation of a new pharaoh in Egypt, Psammetik II, inspired the Jews to think that perhaps here was a warrior strong enough to combat Nebuchadnezzar.

Secret Meetings, Secret Hopes

These hopes, spawned in a sea of discontent and rebellion, culminated in a secret meeting of nations who wished to throw off the yoke of Babylonian oppression. Envoys of the kings of Edom, Moab, Ammon, Tyre, and Judah huddled together to plot their strategy

(Jeremiah 27:3). Even the "prophets" predicted a climactic end to Babylonian domination within two years.

The time seemed right for action, and this top-secret meeting of potential allies discussed the possibility of a united rebellion. Unfortunately for these envoys, God directed Jeremiah to denounce the plot publicly (Jeremiah 27:1–15).

Perhaps Jeremiah's announcement squashed the conspiracy, or perhaps Nebuchadnezzar heard of the plot, but in any case, no organized rebellion took place. Zedekiah remained a loyal vassal king.

William H. Shea has developed a fascinating and logical hypothesis that links the rebellion in Babylon, the summoning of Zedekiah to Babylon, and the convocation on the plain of Dura mentioned in Daniel 3. Shea argues that the assembly on the plain of Dura in the province of Babylon, where delegates from all the other provinces of Babylon had to kneel before a golden image of Nebuchadnezzar or be cast into a fiery furnace, took place in 594 B.C. following the suppression of the revolt. Government officials were required to kneel before the image as a sign of loyalty to Nebuchadnezzar. Nebuchadnezzar also summoned the vassal kings, including Zedekiah,[4] to take part in this ceremony of loyalty.[5]

The final uprising against Babylon began late in 589 B.C. with the enthronement of another new king in Egypt. Pharaoh Apries, or Hophra, encouraged Judah to revolt against Babylon and promised to aid Judah in this attempt. Judah, Ammon, and Tyre all stopped paying tribute to Nebuchadnezzar. The exact causes for

Judah's final revolt are unclear. The Bible is silent, and the Babylonian Chronicle has a gap between 594 and 557 B.C.

Nebuchadnezzar's Third and Final Assault

Nebuchadnezzar's response to this rebellion was swift and harsh.

> In the ninth year of Zedekiah's reign, on the tenth day of the tenth month, Nebuchadnezzar king of Babylon marched against Jerusalem with his whole army. He encamped outside the city and built siege works all around it.
>
> 2 KINGS 25:1

On January 15, 588 B.C., the armies of Babylon reached Jerusalem's walls. This date—the start of Nebuchadnezzar's siege of Jerusalem—marks the beginning of the end for the nation of Judah. The event was so significant that its date was recorded four separate times in various books of the Old Testament.[6]

One by one, Judah's cities and towns fell to Nebuchadnezzar. All the while, the Babylonian king was laying siege to Jerusalem. Soon only three major cities held out against Babylon: Jerusalem, Lachish, and Azekah.

During the long months of siege, the twin specters of famine and disease gripped the people. Mothers killed and ate their children to stay alive, and at least one-third of the people in the city died.[7]

The siege of Jerusalem was temporarily lifted when word came that the Egyptian army was coming to rescue her ally, Judah.[8] Jerusalem was euphoric; people danced in the streets. Deliverance was on its way!

But Jeremiah had an ominous message:

> *"Pharaoh's army, which has marched out to support you, will go back to its own land, to Egypt. Then the Babylonians will return and attack this city; they will capture it and burn it down."*
>
> JEREMIAH 37:7–8

Jeremiah's prophecy was fulfilled all too soon. On July 18, 586 B.C., the Babylonians breached Jerusalem's defenses and poured into the city, ruthlessly butchering another third of its inhabitants.[9] The city had been under siege for over thirty months.

King Zedekiah fled Jerusalem at night and tried to escape toward Ammon on the other side of the Jordan River, "but the Babylonian army pursued the king and overtook him in the plains of Jericho" (2 Kings 25:5). Ammon had been Judah's ally and was still free, but Zedekiah never made it to safety.

Judah Is No More

The age of confrontation ended in disaster. Judah had dared to stand against the power of Babylon, and she was crushed under the onslaught of that mighty war machine. As the final embers died out in the charred ruins that were once her capital city, Judah ceased to exist as an independent nation. The times of the Gentiles had begun.

Babylon was the nation that destroyed God's kingdom on earth. Babylon sacked and burned the temple of Solomon and removed the last king to sit on the throne of David and rule over an independent nation of Israel. Babylonians ripped the people from their promised land and carried them into captivity.

In this chapter of our tale of two cities, Jerusalem moved into the Time of the Gentiles—a period when Israel was without a king from the line of David. The Gentiles would rule the world, including the people of Israel.

Babylon, Iraq—To hear the Iraqi public relations people tell it, this once-mighty city got undeservedly bad press in antiquity. Babylon's image problem—"the mother of harlots and abomination of the Earth"—is largely the fault of the Jews, the promoters say. They bore a grudge against the place ever since being "borne away unto captivity" by King Nebuchadnezzar in the 7th century B.C.

MICHAEL DOBBS, *San Jose Mercury News*[10]

9
History's "Head of Gold"

If the *Jerusalem Post* had been in operation in the autumn of 605 B.C., the headlines might have screamed, "**BABYLON RAPES JUDAH!**"

Nebuchadnezzar swept through the land of Judah, furiously pursuing the fleeing Egyptian army, plundering and pillaging cities and towns as he went. From the simplest villages to the glorious temple, every building was open to Nebuchadnezzar's rage. Palaces and temples surrendered their priceless treasures to Nebuchadnezzar's hordes of invaders, and children of prominent Jews were gathered together and herded to Babylon—captive "guests" of the government.

> *Nebuchadnezzar king of Babylon came to Jerusalem and*
> *besieged it. And the Lord delivered Jehoiakim king of Judah*
> *into his hand, along with some of the articles from the temple*
> *of God. These he carried off to the temple of his god in Baby-*
> *lonia and put in the treasure house of his god. Then the king*
> *ordered Ashpenaz, chief of his court officials, to bring in*
> *some of the Israelites from the royal family and the nobility.*
> DANIEL 1:1–3

The biblical book of Daniel is often viewed as a twisted maze of bizarre dreams and visions. But Daniel did not write his book to confuse anyone. He wrote it to present two important truths.

First, Daniel offers hope for the future. Israel was living in the Time of the Gentiles, the period between the fall of Judah and the coming of the Messiah, and the people needed to know that God had not abandoned them. God's messianic kingdom would still come, Daniel assured them, but its inauguration would be delayed for a little while.

Second, the book of Daniel stresses piety and proper living in the present. By his own example and that of his associates, Daniel instructed the Jews on how to live while waiting for God's kingdom to come.

The first chapter of Daniel introduces four young men of faith who resolve to live godly lives in the pagan culture of Babylon. Chapters 2 through 7 were written not in Hebrew, but in Aramaic, the language of the people from the time of the Captivity. The second and seventh chapters give an overview of Gentile history; the third and sixth chapters tell of persecution and supernatural protection; and the fourth and fifth chapters detail God's revelation to a Gentile kings.

Nebuchadnezzar's Distressing Dream

The second and seventh chapters of Daniel present God's plan for the world following the fall of Judah. The story begins one night when Nebuchadnezzar has a troubling dream.

> *Nebuchadnezzar had dreams; his mind was troubled and he could not sleep. So the king summoned the magicians, enchanters, sorcerers and astrologers to tell him what he had dreamed. When they came in and stood before the king, he said to them, "I have had a dream that troubles me and I want to know what it means."*
>
> *Then the astrologers answered the king in Aramaic, "O king, live forever! Tell your servants the dream, and we will interpret it."*
>
> *The king replied to the astrologers, "This is what I have firmly decided: If you do not tell me what my dream was and interpret it, I will have you cut into pieces and your houses turned into piles of rubble. But if you tell me the dream and explain it, you will receive from me gifts and rewards and great honor. So tell me the dream and interpret it for me."*
>
> *. . . The astrologers answered the king, "There is not a man on earth who can do what the king asks! No king, however great and mighty, has ever asked such a thing of any magician or enchanter or astrologer. What the king asks is too difficult. No one can reveal it to the king except the gods, and they do not live among men."*

This made the king so angry and furious that he ordered the execution of all the wise men of Babylon. So the decree was issued to put the wise men to death, and men were sent to look for Daniel and his friends to put them to death. . . .

At this, Daniel went in to the king and asked for time, so that he might interpret the dream for him. Then Daniel returned to his house and explained the matter to his friends Hananiah, Mishael and Azariah. He urged them to plead for mercy from the God of heaven concerning this mystery. . . . During the night the mystery was revealed to Daniel in a vision. . . .

The king asked Daniel (also called Belteshazzar), "Are you able to tell me what I saw in my dream and interpret it?"

Daniel replied, "No wise man, enchanter, magician or diviner can explain to the king the mystery he has asked about, but there is a God in heaven who reveals mysteries. He has shown King Nebuchadnezzar what will happen in days to come. Your dream and the visions that passed through your mind as you lay on your bed are these:

"As you were lying there, O king, your mind turned to things to come, and the revealer of mysteries showed you what is going to happen. . . . You looked, O king, and there before you stood a large statue—an enormous, dazzling statue, awesome in appearance. The head of the statue was made of pure gold, its chest and arms of silver, its belly and thighs of bronze, its legs of iron, its feet partly of iron and partly of baked clay. While you were watching, a rock was cut out, but not by human hands. It struck the statue on its feet of iron and clay and smashed them. Then the iron, the clay, the bronze, the silver and the gold were broken to pieces at the same time and became like chaff on a threshing floor

*in the summer. The wind swept them away without leaving a
trace. But the rock that struck the statue became a huge
mountain and filled the whole earth.*

*. . . "You, O king, are the king of kings. The God of
heaven has given you dominion and power and might and
glory. . . . You are that head of gold."*

From the book of DANIEL, chapter 2

The Dream's Significance

The statue in Nebuchadnezzar's dream contained
four different metals representing the Gentile kingdoms that would rise to rule the earth. For the first
time since the formation of the nation of Israel, God
was handing control of the inhabited world over to the
Gentile nations. The first metal, the head of gold, was
Nebuchadnezzar's Babylon.

The other Gentile powers, though not specifically
named by Daniel, can be determined. The "chest and
arms of silver" represented a second world empire that
would rise after Babylon. Babylon was replaced on the
world scene by Medo-Persia, and this was the next
world empire to hold sway over the land of Israel.

The third portion of the statue was the "belly and
thighs of bronze"; and Daniel interpreted this to mean
that "a third kingdom, one of bronze, will rule over the
whole earth" (2:39). The power that replaced the Medo-
Persian Empire was the kingdom of Greece led by Alexander the Great.

The fourth empire was made of iron. It represented
the final Gentile empire ruling over Israel when the

Messiah would come to restore God's kingdom on earth. The empire that supplanted the Greeks and ruled over Judah at the time of Christ's first coming was Rome. Rome was the fourth and final Gentile power in Daniel's vision.

Other Gentile powers had existed before Babylon, of course. Some of them, Egypt and Assyria, for instance, had even dominated the land of Israel. Yet it was Babylon who first achieved total supremacy over God's kingdom ruled by the line of David and who thus became the first in a series of Gentile powers to rule the world. No king from the line of David has ruled over Israel since Babylon's victory.

Israel will not rule over the earth again until the Time of the Gentiles is completed. Daniel saw a rock quarried without human hands that struck the statue and disintegrated it. This rock then grew into a mountain and filled the earth. The meaning of the rock gave Daniel great hope:

> *"The God of heaven will set up a kingdom that will never be destroyed, nor will it be left to another people. It will crush all those kingdoms and bring them to an end, but it will itself endure forever."*
> DANIEL 2:44

God has a plan for His people Israel, but that plan will not be made evident until the Time of the Gentiles is completed. Then God will intervene to set up His kingdom on earth.

Then King Nebuchadnezzar fell prostrate before Daniel and paid him honor and ordered that an offering and incense be presented to him. The king said to Daniel, "Surely your God is the God of gods and the Lord of kings and a revealer of mysteries, for you were able to reveal this mystery."
DANIEL 2:46–47

Daniel's Dream

Daniel was not done with dreams. Long after Nebuchadnezzar had died, when Babylon's final king, Belshazzar, had assumed the throne, Daniel himself had a troubling dream:

"In my vision at night I looked, and there before me were the four winds of heaven churning up the great sea. Four great beasts, each different from the others, came up out of the sea.

"The first was like a lion, and it had the wings of an eagle. I watched until its wings were torn off and it was lifted from the ground so that it stood on two feet like a man, and the heart of a man was given to it.

"And there before me was a second beast, which looked like a bear. It was raised up on one of its sides, and it had three ribs in its mouth between its teeth. It was told, 'Get up and eat your fill of flesh!'

"After that, I looked, and there before me was another beast, one that looked like a leopard. And on its back it had four wings like those of a bird. This beast had four heads, and it was given authority to rule.

"After that, in my vision at night I looked, and there before me was a fourth beast—terrifying and frightening

and very powerful. It had large iron teeth; it crushed and devoured its victims and trampled underfoot whatever was left. It was different from all the former beasts, and it had ten horns.

"While I was thinking about the horns, there before me was another horn, a little one, which came up among them; and three of the first horns were uprooted before it. This horn had eyes like the eyes of a man and a mouth that spoke boastfully. . . .

"Then I continued to watch because of the boastful words the horn was speaking. I kept looking until the beast was slain and its body destroyed and thrown into the blazing fire. (The other beasts had been stripped of their authority, but were allowed to live for a period of time.)

"In my vision at night I looked, and there before me was one like a son of man, coming with the clouds of heaven. . . . He was given authority, glory and sovereign power; all peoples, nations and men of every language worshiped him. His dominion is an everlasting dominion that will not pass away, and his kingdom is one that will never be destroyed."

DANIEL 7:2–8, 11–14

Daniel's dream is similar to Nebuchadnezzar's dream, but now the four successive Gentile powers are pictured as four ferocious beasts coming up out of the sea to rule the earth. God Himself told Daniel that "the four great beasts are four kingdoms that will rise from the earth" (Daniel 7:17).

The first beast, Babylon, is described as a lion with the wings of an eagle. Statues of winged, human-headed bulls or lions have been found in the region of Assyria.

They are pagan representations of angelic beings. Perhaps this picture illustrates Nebuchadnezzar's pride. But in Daniel's vision, the beast's wings are torn off, much as Nebuchadnezzar himself was humbled.[1]

Daniel described the second beast, Medo-Persia, as a rather lopsided bear with three ribs in its mouth. This is a perfect picture of the Medo-Persian Empire—an empire composed of two countries, but with the Persians more dominant than the Medes. The three ribs in the bear's mouth graphically illustrate the three prominent conquests of the empire: Lydia in 546 B.C., Babylon in 539 B.C., and Egypt in 525 B.C.

The third beast, Greece, is pictured as a leopard with four wings and four heads. The wings portray the swift flight of the Greek empire as it expanded rapidly to the east under Alexander the Great. The four heads represent the division of the empire following Alexander's death. Four generals carved up the empire: Ptolemy I took Israel and Egypt, Seleucus I took Syria and Mesopotamia, Lysimachus took Thrace and Asia Minor, and Cassander took Macedonia and Greece.

Daniel described the four-way division again in chapter 8: "The shaggy goat is the king of Greece, and the large horn between his eyes is the first king. The four horns that replaced the one that was broken off represent four kingdoms that will emerge from his nation but will not have the same power" (Daniel 8:21–22).

The fourth beast, Rome, is shadowy and scary! It is "terrifying and frightening and very powerful." It destroys and stamps out opposition, and it is different from all the other beasts. By using iron to describe the beast's teeth, Daniel links the beast to the fourth part of the statue in Nebuchadnezzar's dream. The fourth empire is more terrifying than its predecessors. It is the empire that will hold sway when the Messiah comes.

Both of Daniel's dreams pointed toward a long and dark tunnel for the people of Abraham. The Time of the Gentiles would bring difficulty for the Jewish people as they experienced persecution and trouble because of their faith in God. Still, in both dreams, there is light and victory at the end of the tunnel. That light is the coming kingdom of God that would spell the end of the Time of the Gentiles and the beginning of God's rule on earth.

10
The King Who Ate Grass

Although the dreams of both Daniel and Nebuchadnezzar foretold the ultimate victory of the people of Israel, they also predicted a time when nations who did not know God would rule the earth. This period would be known as the Time of the Gentiles.

What nation headed the list in the Time of the Gentiles? Who stood first in line of the Gentile powers attempting to usurp God's program for His people?

Babylon!

Two Images of a Nation

When Daniel wrote the fourth and fifth chapters of his book, it is as if he had searched through his seventy-year-old Babylonian scrapbook to find two pictures to represent all that was the nation of Babylon. The first picture comes from Nebuchadnezzar's time, early in Daniel's lifetime. The second snapshot comes from the time of King Belshazzar. It provides a glimpse of Babylon on the final night of its existence as a nation.

Nebuchadnezzar reigned for forty-three years, from 605 to 562 B.C. Only fragments of the Babylonian Chronicle, Babylon's official court record, have survived, and for most of Nebuchadnezzar's life we have no record of his specific actions. But the fourth chapter of Daniel records a seven-year period in Nebuchadnezzar's life when God made him insane.

This revealing portrait of Nebuchadnezzar begins by describing the greatness of his kingdom. He had reached the pinnacle of power, but he had never been able to overcome one obstacle: pride. Instead of ascribing his greatness to the God he had recognized as the "God of gods" when Daniel revealed the meaning of his dream, Nebuchadnezzar considered himself his own source of greatness.

On the brick wall towards the north my heart inspired me to build a palace for the protecting of Babylon. I built there a palace like the palace of Babylon of brick and bitumen. . . . I raised its summit and connected it with the palace with brick and bitumen. I made it high as a mountain. Mighty cedar trunks I laid on it for roof. Double doors of cedar wood overlaid with copper, thresholds and hinges made of bronze did I set up in its doorways. That building I named "May Nebuchadnezzar live, may he grow old as restorer of Esagila."

AN ANCIENT INSCRIPTION ABOUT THE BUILDING OF NEBUCHADNEZZAR'S PALACE ON THE NORTHERN EDGE OF BABYLON[1]

One night Nebuchadnezzar was walking on the roof of his royal palace, very likely the southern palace located just inside the inner-city walls between the Procession Street and the Euphrates River. From his vantage point, he could look over his throne room, the royal living area, the courtyards, and living and working space for his vast inner circle of government workers. Next to the palace he could see the famous hanging gardens.

Nebuchadnezzar admired the city of Babylon and reflected on how it mirrored his greatness. Full of his own importance, he exclaimed, "Is not this the great Babylon I have built as the royal residence, by my mighty power and for the glory of my majesty?" (Daniel 4:30).

No doubt about it—Babylon was majestic. Nebuchadnezzar had buried the Ishtar Gate built by his father so he could construct a new (and far more magnificent!) Ishtar Gate on top of it. He rebuilt the southern palace, constructed the hanging gardens, repaired the walls around the city, restored the Tower of Babel and the temple to Marduk, and built or extensively repaired most of the other temples in the city. His building exploits were legendary. On many of the bricks he had made for his building projects he stamped the following inscription: "I am Nebuchadnezzar, king of Babylon, king of everything from sea to far sea."

Because my heart did not wish the dwelling place of my Majesty to be in another place, because I did not build a royal dwelling in any other place, and because I did not consign the kingly property to all lands, my dwelling place in Babylon grew insufficient for the dignity of my Majesty.

AN ANCIENT INSCRIPTION DESCRIBING ONE OF NEBUCHAD-NEZZAR'S DWELLING PLACES[2]

Nebuchadnezzar's boasting was not false, but it was prideful. God struck Nebuchadnezzar with insanity, and for seven years, the mighty king ate grass like cattle. People chased him away, and "his body was drenched with the dew. . . . His hair grew like the feathers of an eagle and his nails like the claws of a bird" (Daniel 4:33).

Nebuchadnezzar's punishment lasted until he admitted that "the Most High is sovereign over the kingdoms of men and gives them to anyone he wishes" (Daniel 4:32). Like his predecessors at the Tower of Babel, the king of Babylon learned that his greatest achievements fell far short when measured against God's majesty.

Babylon's Demise

The final kings of Babylon were but shadows of Nebuchadnezzar's power and splendor. Nabonidus

Satellite image of Babylon from 423 miles above
the earth.

① Artificial hill with Hussein's Palace

② Procession Street

③ Palace of Nebuchadnezzar

④ Ninmach temple

⑤ Saddam Hussein Guest House

⑥ Rebuilt temples

⑦ Restored Greek theater

⑧ Ruins of Tower of Babel

⑨ Artificial hill built by Saddam Hussein in 1988

⑩ Canal follows outline of ancient city walls

⑪ Artificial hill built by Saddam Hussein in 1988

▲
The Saddam Hussein Guest House, located in the center of Babylon.

Reconstruction of the Ninmach temple viewed from the Ishtar Gate.
▼

▲

A close-up view of the northern hill.

① Saddam Hussein's new palace built on artificial hill

② Nebuchadnezzar's rebuilt palace

③ Saddam Hussein Guest House

This picture was taken in Babylon by Reverend Arthur Blessitt in 1998 and is used with his permission. The building in the background is Saddam Husein's new palace that overlooks the rebuilt palace of King Nebuchadnezzar.

▼

▲
The walls of Babylon are built on the original foundations.

◀ Rebuilding of some of the ruins of Nebuchadnezzar's palace.

Entrance to Nebuchadnezzar's palace at night.
▼

A close-up view of the eastern hill, surrounded by a large resovoir.

A close-up of the southern hill, with the Euphrates River at the bottom.

▲

Reconstruction of the ancient Greek theater

Looking at the restored Greek theater.

▼

Poster for the Babylon International Festival featuring
Saddam Hussein and King Nebuchadnezzar.

FROM **NABUKHADNEZZAR** TO **SADDAM HUSSEIN**

BABYLON UNDERGOES A RENAISSANCE

BABYLON INTERNATIONAL FESTIVAL

FROM SEPTEMBER 22 TO OCTOBER 22 1987

SILCO _ BAGHDAD

Mural in Babylon depicting Nebuchadnezzar leading his army against the city of Jerusalem. Saddam Hussein seeks to destroy the modern nation of Israel.

▲

The rebuilt walls of the Procession Street rise from the ruins of ancient Babylon.

On the opening night of the Babylon Festival children march down the Procession Street carrying palm branches in celebration.

▼

▲
A model of the "Tower of Babel" ziggurat whose reconstruction is planned by the government of Iraq.

The Euphrates River still flows through Babylon.
▼

Saddam Hussein's half-size reconstruction of the Ishtar Gate.

A portrait of Saddam Hussein greets visitors entering the city of Samarra. Portraits of Hussein are everywhere in Iraq.

In this seal it's hard to miss the linking of Nebuchadnezzar, the famed biblical ruler of Babylon and Saddam Hussein.

▲

American-made tanks captured from the Iranians during the Iran-Iraq war.

A proud display of more than sixty thousand rifles captured from Iran in the closing months of the Iran-Iraq war. An American-made tank (not pictured) was given a special place of "honor" among the spoils of war.

▼

Children in Iraqi Pioneer uniforms at a ceremony in Baghdad. The design on their uniforms is a map of the Arab world.

ascended the throne in 556 B.C., but he preferred rebuilding temples in the distant cities of Haran and Tema to governing the people of Babylon. For ten years he stayed out of town, and his son, Belshazzar, ruled in his stead.

Belshazzar inherited Nebuchadnezzar's pride, but unfortunately he did not inherit his grandfather's administrative and military abilities. King Cyrus of Persia moved to capture the Babylonian Empire, and in late September or early October, 539 B.C., Cyrus defeated Babylon's army on the Tigris River just south of modern-day Baghdad. On October 10, Cyrus captured the city of Sippar, just forty miles north of Babylon, and two days later, on October 12, the Babylonian Chronicle reports that "the army of Cyrus entered Babylon without a battle."[3]

How could a supposedly impregnable city fall in a matter of hours without a battle? The present government of Iraq blames the fall on a plot between the Jews and Persians: As I heard an Iraqi official say at the Babylon Festival, "It was not until Cyrus had collaborated with the Jews inside the city" that he was able to tighten the siege around the city and subsequently to occupy it.[4]

It was the Persians who destroyed Nebuchadnezzar's magnificent city in 539 B.C. According to Salam Yacoub, the guide from the Iraqi Ministry of Information, they managed to capture Babylon because of the treachery of the Jewish community. Tipped off by the Jews, the Persians built earth dams to block the nearby Euphrates, thus depriving the city of its natural defenses.

MICHAEL DOBBS in the *San Jose Mercury News*[5]

While such a view of history may serve Saddam Hussein's political ends, it does not square with the facts. The official Babylonian court record simply says that the Persian army entered Babylon on October 12, two days after capturing Sippar, and captured the city without a battle.

The ancient historian Herodotus provides additional information. Cyrus diverted the water of the Euphrates River into a canal upriver from Babylon so that the water level dropped "to the height of the middle of a man's thigh." The Persian army knew that on this particular night the Babylonians were "making merry at a festival," so the walls would be poorly defended.[6]

Belshazzar's Last Party

While the Persians were watching the water level drop, the festival inside Babylon was in full swing. King Belshazzar was giving a banquet for a thousand of his nobles, probably in the throne room and adjacent courtyard of Nebuchadnezzar's southern palace.

For the Babylon Festivals I attended, the throne room was used for musical concerts. Hundreds could sit comfortably in the room in spite of the large stage constructed for the performers. As I sat and listened to music, I could almost visualize Belshazzar and his thousand nobles crowded into that regal room on that fateful night.

Perhaps to steel his commanders for the anticipated siege, Belshazzar focused their attention on Babylon's past victories. He gave orders to bring in the gold and silver goblets that Nebuchadnezzar had taken from the temple in Jerusalem, so that he and his nobles, his wives, and his concubines could drink from them.

It is easy to imagine him raising a golden goblet, exalting himself and his gods as he gloated over his grandfather's victory seventy years earlier. As he and his nobles desecrated the articles that had been dedicated to the God of Israel, "they praised the gods of gold and silver, of bronze, iron, wood and stone" (Daniel 5:4).

Belshazzar's prideful party did not last the night. Even as he stood with the cup to his lips, the fingers of a man's hand appeared and began writing on the wall. Terrified, Belshazzar summoned his wise men to interpret the riddle of the writing. No one had any idea what it meant. But then someone remembered an old man named Daniel who had solved impossible mysteries in Nebuchadnezzar's time.

Belshazzar summoned Daniel and offered him the position of "third highest ruler in the kingdom" if Daniel could interpret the message (Daniel 5:16). This was the highest position Belshazzar could offer. He himself was the second highest ruler since his father, Nabonidus, was still alive.

Daniel rejected Belshazzar's pompous offer, but he agreed to interpret the mysterious message. First, however, he taught Belshazzar a history lesson. Daniel reminded the king how God judged Nebuchadnezzar's pride by removing his sanity and driving him from his throne for seven years. Daniel concluded, "But you his [grand]son, O Belshazzar, have not humbled yourself, though you knew all this. Instead you have set yourself up against the Lord of heaven" (verses 22–23).

Daniel now explained the handwriting on the wall. "God has numbered the days of your reign and brought it to an end," Daniel told Belshazzar. "You have been weighed on the scales and found wanting. . . . Your kingdom is divided and given to the Medes and Persians" (verses 5:26–28).

The news was grim, but Belshazzar kept his word. Daniel was hailed, dressed in purple, adorned with a gold chain, and declared third highest ruler in the kingdom. The kingdom, however, fell before morning.

The Persians slipped along the riverbank and entered a side gate that led into the southern palace. In the very brief battle that followed, Belshazzar and a few of the nobles were killed. Babylon fell to the Medo-Persians.

Babylon, the head of gold, no longer ruled the nations.

11
Conquered but Not Destroyed

If we read the Bible, we know that Babylon fell to the invading Medo-Persians. If we read the newspapers, we know that Saddam Hussein is trying to restore the glory of ancient Babylon even as his kingdom is threatened with invasion. But whatever happened to Babylon during the intervening twenty-five hundred years? Did the city of man continue its war against the City of God? Or was it completely destroyed, apparently never to rise again?

What Happened to Babylon?

If our tale of two cities ended when Judah fell, it would seem as though the city of man had triumphed over the City of God. But the same prideful rebellion that caused confusion at Babel also brought about the fall of Babylon's kings. Babylon was like a haughty princess, tossing her head and proclaiming, "I did it my way."

Babylon occupied the world's center stage for only about two generations. The city rose to fame in 612 B.C. when Babylonian armies destroyed the city of Nineveh, and Babylon supplanted Assyria as the dominant power in the Middle East. Less than a century later, in 539 B.C., Babylon was conquered by Medo-Persia and gradually slipped back into obscurity.

Seventeen days after Babylon fell to Cyrus's general, Cyrus himself entered the city. The average person in Babylon would not have noticed any major changes in daily affairs. Cyrus established Babylon as one of his capital cities and assumed the title "King of Babylon."[1] He wisely tried to establish peace and to restore a sense of normality and order in the city.[2]

When I entered Babylon as a friend and [when] I established the seat of the government in the palace of the ruler under jubilation and rejoicing, Marduk, the great lord, [induced] the magnanimous inhabitants of Babylon [to love me], and I was daily endeavoring to worship him. My numerous troops walked around in Babylon in peace, I did not allow anybody to terrorize [any place] of the [country of Sumer] and Akkad. I strove for peace in Babylon and in all his [other] sacred cities.

CYRUS, King of Babylon[3]

Babylon remained at peace throughout the reign of Cyrus and his successor, Cambyses. Following the death of Cambyses, Darius I assumed control of the Medo-Persian Empire. The citizens of Babylon rebelled against Darius, and he was forced to recapture the city on two separate occasions. After his second suppression of a revolt, Herodotus reports that "Darius destroyed their walls and reft away all their gates, neither of which things Cyrus had done at the first taking of Babylon."[4]

Though Babylon had fallen into difficult times, it continued to be an important and active city under the reign of the Medo-Persians.

The Empire of Bronze

In 334 B.C., Alexander the Great and the Greeks, bent on conquest, crossed the Hellespont separating Europe from Asia. In a series of rapid and stunning defeats, the Medo-Persian Empire collapsed before Alexander. In just eleven years, Alexander and his army conquered the then-known world.

Arriving at Babylon after having run roughshod over the Medo-Persian Empire, Alexander made great plans for the city to become the eastern capital of his empire. He set men to work rebuilding and enlarging the temple of Marduk and the ziggurat in the center of the city.⁵ He began preparing the Euphrates as a major shipping port. He had a harbor dug that was large enough for a thousand warships, and he built dockyards on it.⁶ Unfortunately, Alexander died when he was only thirty-two years old, long before he could complete all his ambitious projects.

The Bronze Empire Splits

Following Alexander's death, the Greek Empire broke into four parts, just as Daniel had predicted. Macedonia and Greece, Alexander's original empire, went to Cassander. Lysimachus grabbed Thrace and Asia Minor. Judah and Egypt went to Ptolemy I; and Syria, Mesopotamia, and Medo-Persia went to Seleucus I.

Seleucus I, more than any other individual, was responsible for the gradual decline of the city of Babylon. Though he took the title "King of Babylon," he was repeatedly forced to take and retake the city as he fought to assert his authority over the region. He finally decided to establish a new capital on the Tigris River about forty-five miles north of Babylon, and he named the city after himself. With the establishment of Seleucia, the government and trade center shifted from Babylon on the Euphrates to Seleucia on the Tigris. Babylon never regained its prominent role in the region.

Though Babylon was no longer a leader among cities, it did not cease to exist. The temple of Marduk and the other temples in Babylon were still in operation, and Babylon remained the dominant religious center in the area.

Sometime during the Greek period, a theater was built in Babylon. This theater, now rebuilt by the government of Iraq, can hold up to four thousand people, suggesting that the city still had a sizable population when the theater was constructed.

Babylon Limps Along

Parthians replaced the Greeks as rulers in Mesopotamia in 139 B.C., and they continued to control this area through the time of the Romans. The Parthians built another city next to Seleucia and named it Ctesiphon. These three cities vied for power. Ctesiphon became the political center, Seleucia remained the business and trading center, and Babylon continued as the religious center of Mesopotamia.

Seleucia at the present time has become larger than Babylon, whereas the greater part of Babylon is so deserted that one would not hesitate to say what one of the comic poets said in reference to the Megalopolitans in Arcadia: "The Great City has become a great desert."
STRABO[7]

Babylon was not totally deserted, but Seleucia was now more densely populated, and large sections of Babylon were no longer inhabited. Babylon still existed, but the city was only a shell of its former glory.

Josephus provides an interesting piece of information about Babylon in the century before Christ. In 40 B.C., the Parthians extended their empire west to Syria and joined forces with elements in Judah who were trying to remove from power Hyrcanus, the pro-Roman Jewish high priest. Hyrcanus was captured, mutilated, and deported to Parthia. Josephus records that the king of Parthia later treated Hyrcanus kindly and "set him free from his bonds, and gave him a habitation at Babylon, where there were Jews in great numbers."[8]

Babylon in the Time of the Romans

The New Testament likewise gives evidence that many Jews lived in and near Babylon in the first century A.D. On the Day of Pentecost a large number of Jews were gathered in Jerusalem from "every nation under heaven" (Acts 2:5). These included Jews from the Gulf region, among them "Parthians, Medes and Elamites; residents of Mesopotamia" (2:9). Some of these Jews undoubtedly lived in Babylon.

In 1 Peter 5:13, Peter sends a greeting that has puzzled people for centuries: "She who is in Babylon, chosen together with you, sends you her greetings." Who was "she"?

It is likely that "she" refers to the church in Babylon. The word "church" is a feminine noun, so if Peter wanted to refer to the church as a single body, he would use the pronoun "she" instead of "it."

If Jews lived in Babylon and some of them heard the gospel on the Day of Pentecost, it is not hard to imagine that Peter, the Apostle to the Jews, would have journeyed to Babylon to share Christ with the Jews still living there. Most likely, he wrote the first epistle of Peter from Babylon.

Following the end of the New Testament period, information on the existence of Babylon becomes extremely scarce. Many scholars cite Dio, who wrote that when Trajan visited Babylon in A.D. 116 he saw "nothing but mounds and stones and ruins."[9] But Pausanias wrote that the temple of Bel (Marduk) and the walls were still standing, though most of the city was abandoned.[10]

One traveler who visited Babylon during the Middle Ages was a Jew known as Benjamin of Tudela. He journeyed through the region in the twelfth century and then wrote an account of his travels. Benjamin made two important observations: first, he reported that ten thousand Jews lived in the village of Al Hillah six miles from Babylon; second, he noted that the Jews had an active "Synagogue of Daniel" in Babylon one mile from the ruins of Nebuchadnezzar's temple, probably the temple of Marduk.[11]

Pilgrims as Tourists

In the later Middle Ages, Western pilgrims began making the arduous trek through the Holy Land and beyond, some traveling as far as Mesopotamia. These travelers often kept diaries of their journeys. These sources, however, can be unreliable, because the visitors were at the mercy of local guides who were anxious to show them whatever they wanted to see, whether or not the place was nearby or the site known. The pilgrims were desperate to see significant sites, and the local inhabitants were more than happy to oblige, for a price!

On the day I visited, there were no other tourists, only a handful of Bedouin hustlers lurking in slivers of shade cast by freestanding pillars. One of them grasped my sleeve and unfolded his fist to reveal a tiny cuneiform tablet and a statuette of a Babylonian king. "Very ancient, very real," he said. And very cheap at only $10.

TONY HORWITZ in the *Washington Post*[12]

In 1616 Pietro Della Valle visited the site of the ancient city. He described the ruins of the Tower of Babel and confirmed Koldewey's later report that villagers were mining and selling Babylon's kiln-fired bricks.

Between 1899 and 1912 the German archaeologist Robert Koldewey visited Babylon and began studying its ruins. Koldewey named four Arab villages situated on the site—Kweiresh, Djumdjumma, Sindjar, and Ananeh.[13] Babylon was still inhabited even in Koldewey's time, and had been for some time before his arrival.

When I first traveled to Babylon in 1987, I had an opportunity to see the village of Kweiresh. It was located next to the reconstruction of Nebuchadnezzar's southern palace and just north of the Saddam Hussein Guest House. One year later, though, government officials forced the village to move. Between 1987 and 1988, the government of Iraq had built a large hill just to the west of the southern palace between the palace and the

Euphrates River. I was told at the time by a government official that the hill would become part of a monorail system that would extend above the city of Babylon. In reality, the hill was built as a platform for Saddam Hussein's magnificent palace in Babylon—a palace that allows him to look out over the city he has begun to restore. It was obvious to me that the government wanted to make the city of Babylon more glorious and that the humble village of Kweiresh had to sacrifice some of its land in the process.

Babylon Has Never Been Abandoned

I can find no time in history when it can be said conclusively that Babylon ceased to exist. Her population has risen and fallen through the ages, but there has never been a time when the city has been completely abandoned. Babylon declined in importance after the establishment of Seleucia, Ctesiphon, and Baghdad, but it retained its significance as a religious center. The worship of Marduk and other Babylonian religions continued through the centuries.

Even in this modern era, there are villages around Babylon. Until the early 1980s, the city existed as a small shell of its former glory, but now the government of Iraq has determined to revive and restore the majesty of Babylon. Babylon's fortunes have declined, but the city has never been destroyed.

12
The Two Tyrants

Looking back over his life of conquest, few could have imagined that one born in the tiny village of Tikrit along the banks of the Tigris River could achieve such international notoriety. But even as a young man he aspired to greatness, and his cunning and bravery propelled him into ever higher positions of leadership. His burning ambition was to unify the Arab nations under his leadership. It wasn't long before countries of the West, fearing the consequences of an Arab expansionist policy, formed a multinational force and deployed it in the Middle East against the Arab leader.

Saddam Hussein? No. Saladin, the greatest Muslim

warrior of the twelfth century. His capture of Jerusalem in 1187 caused the Third Crusade.

Another Son of Tikrit

Nearly eight hundred years later, in the same tiny village of Tikrit, Saddam Hussein was born, a man whose passions and methods baffle Americans. We cannot understand why this man invaded the neighboring country of Kuwait that supported him in his eight-year war with Iran. We cannot fathom why he was unwilling to withdraw his troops in the face of worldwide condemnation. We cannot comprehend his barbaric use of chemical weapons on the citizens of his own country, including defenseless women and children. We cannot imagine how he can so brazenly lie to the world about his stockpiling of weapons of mass destruction.

His country is a police state where Iraqis have been arrested for turning off a television when Saddam's image was on the screen or accidentally knocking over one of his ubiquitous posters.[1] Can such a prideful, barbaric leader be sane?

Yes, Saddam Hussein's actions are only too logical. He is not a mentally deranged sociopath. In fact, he is a cold, calculating, rational individual who is following a definite plan.

In an interview, Saddam Hussein was asked to comment on his "Butcher of Baghdad" nickname. "Weakness doesn't assure achieving the objectives required by a leader," he replied.[2]

A Living History

To understand Saddam Hussein's plans and motives, we must first understand something of the Middle East's religious and political history.

The Muslim religion began in the seventh century A.D. with the rise of the prophet Mohammed, who began preaching in the city of Mecca in what today is Saudi Arabia. The people of Mecca opposed his preaching, and he fled from Mecca to Medina in A.D. 622. Called the *Hegira,* this flight is so important to Muslims that their calendar, instead of using B.C. and A.D., begins dating the modern era from the year 622.

Mohammed won a following at Medina, and in A.D. 630 he returned to Mecca in triumph. Seven years later, Arab forces defeated the Persians at the battle of *Al Qadisiyah,* and Islam spread into Iraq and Persia.

Those early centuries were times of vigor and triumph for Islam and for the Arabs. Great leaders such as Saladin were able to galvanize the people and spur them on to further conquest.

But while Islam continued to spread, the political unity of those who were Muslims began to disintegrate. The Egyptians, Turks, Persians, and Arabs developed different spheres of influence and fought for control of the Islamic world.

The glory and prominence of Iraq under Saladin vanished under the heavy hand of foreign domination. In 1534 the Ottoman Turks conquered Iraq and established dominion there that lasted nearly four hundred years, until the end of World War I.

The Turks were Muslims, but they were not Arabs. In World War I, the Ottoman Empire sided with Germany, and after the war, the victorious Allies parceled out much of the Turkish territory. Britain and France randomly divided up the Middle East. The borders of Kuwait, Saudi Arabia, Jordan, Syria, and Iraq are little more than straight lines drawn on a map by the British. Iraq was free of the Turks, but it was still being ruled by foreigners.

The remainder of the twentieth century proved a time of continued foreign domination and national humiliation for the Arabs. Though several Arab countries gained nominal independence, their governments were still heavily influenced by Western powers. In 1948 the United Nations ignored Arab threats and protests and created the nation of Israel. The Holy Land became anything but peaceful.

The Middle East is the world's deadliest neighborhood. It has 17 Arab countries and a Persian republic populated by 231 million Muslims as well as small Christian minorities and one Jewish state with a population of less than 5 million. It has known few days of true peace in this century, none since Israel was born to a rattle of gunfire. . . . Lurching from crisis to moments of ill-conceived optimism and back into crisis, it has spent more on weapons, fought more wars and suffered more casualties than any other part of the Third World.

DAVID LAMB in the *Los Angeles Times*[3]

Israel Not Welcome in the Land

Arabs took the formation of Israel as an insult and declared war against the new state. Israel courageously fought off the combined armies of five Arab states, and after the war ended, Israel had more land than it had been granted under the original United Nations plan!

Israel will not pay anything. We will not make the smallest concession in order to satisfy what you call moderate, or nonmoderate Arab countries.

We have one interest. We want to live here peacefully and defend our lives. We will pay no price to anyone.

ARIEL SHARON[4]

In the 1950s, General Gamal Abdel Nasser rose in Egypt and called for Arabs to unite against Western powers and Israel. He nationalized the Suez Canal in 1956 and closed the Gulf of Aqaba. Britain, France, and Israel responded by attacking Egypt. Again, Arab aspirations were thwarted.

In 1967 Nasser and the Syrians threatened once more to invade Israel, but Israel struck first and humiliated the Arab nations on all sides in the Six Day War. Nasser's dream of a unified Arab nation was shattered.

Jerusalem is not negotiable. It will never be negotiable. Jerusalem is the heart of the Jews. It has been the capital of the Jews for the last 3,000 years. We will accept no other arrangement.

ARIEL SHARON[5]

Arabs Search for a Leader

Current conflicts in the Middle East are not the product of spontaneous combustion but the natural result of passions, hatred, and rivalries that have simmered for centuries. The Arab people feel that their great past has given way to a demeaning present. They blame much of this on the domination they have experienced by Western powers including Turkey, Britain, and now the United States. They are looking for a leader who will throw off the domination of the West and lead them back to the greatness they once had.

Those who live in the Middle East have a stronger sense of history than Americans do. Some houses in the Middle East were standing when the first Europeans set foot in America! The Arab "identity crisis" and the Arabs' keen sense of history help explain the current upheaval in the Middle East.

The Iraqi Nation and Its President

I say with my heart full of sadness that there is not yet in Iraq an Iraqi people.

FAISAL I, the first king of modern Iraq, in 1932[6]

Iraq, which in 1932 was the first Arab nation to gain its independence from British control, is a country without a clear identity. Twenty percent of the people are Kurds, a non-Arab group whom Saddam attacked with a lethal cocktail of chemical weapons after rebellions in 1987–88. Westerners had a difficult time understanding how Hussein could poison his own people, but in fact, though the Kurds were Iraqi, they were not Arab.

In 1937, Saddam Hussein was born in the village of Tikrit, about a hundred miles north of Baghdad on the Tigris River. Though he attended secondary school in Baghdad and law school in Cairo, his real education came from the crowd of zealous revolutionaries with whom he hung out on the streets.

Another guiding influence was his uncle, Khayrallah Tulfah. Khayrallah raised Saddam and later arranged for him to marry one of his daughters. When Saddam came to power, Khayrallah was rewarded by being named mayor of Baghdad. Khayrallah Tulfah, whose influence on Saddam was significant, was not exactly open-minded about non-Arabs. He once published a booklet titled *Three Whom God Should Not Have Created: Persians, Jews, and Flies.*

Saddam Hussein's early exploits on behalf of the Baath Party have been elevated to the status of legend. At twenty-two, he was chosen to lead what was an unsuccessful assassination attempt against the president of Iraq. He escaped to Egypt, returned to Iraq in 1963 when the Baath Party first came to power, was imprisoned from 1964 to 1966 when the Baath government was toppled in a coup, and then escaped from prison.

When the Baath Party again seized control in 1968, Saddam Hussein became, at age thirty-one, a leader in Iraq. Under the patronage of his older cousin al-Bakr, Saddam became deputy chairman of the Revolutionary Command Council in 1969 and deputy secretary-general of the Baath Party in 1977. Later he was named vice-chairman of the Revolutionary Command Council, the nine-member body that legislates by decree.

A few weeks after becoming president of Iraq in 1979, Saddam Hussein executed some of his closest friends and fellow members of the ruling Baath Party. Videotapes of the meeting at which the "traitors" were named show Hussein reading their names from a list, pausing to puff on a cigar while members of his audience squirmed in their seats.[7] Once their names were called, the supposed conspirators were marched off and killed. Saddam Hussein had begun his pattern of rule by force.

Iraq today is one of the most paranoid nations in the world. When I traveled in Iraq as an invited guest, our group was assigned an official "watcher" who dogged our footsteps. On at least one occasion we were asked to surrender the film in our cameras, though we had taken pictures only of an innocent village. When some of us balked at handing over our film, we were taken to a police station and simply held there until we gave in.

Babylon is once again part of a police state, where individual liberties are almost nonexistent and the country's leaders use power and force to rule. Power and force—just as in the days of Nebuchadnezzar.

The Call for Arab Nationalism

The Baath Party to which Saddam Hussein belongs was formed to promote pan-Arab nationalism. The party's goal is to unify the Arab people and elevate them as a race. By pointing to the past, the Baath Party reminds

Arabs both of the greatness they once experienced and of the Western invaders who stripped them of that greatness.

The glory of the Arabs stems from the glory of Iraq. Throughout history, whenever Iraq became mighty and flourished, so did the Arab nation. This is why we are striving to make Iraq mighty, formidable, able and developed.
SADDAM HUSSEIN in 1979[8]

An ominous example of this mentality is the current description of the United States military presence in the Persian Gulf region. Many Muslims refer to the U.S. armed forces as "crusaders." This is not a compliment. To the Muslims it recalls the armies of Western infidels that attacked, conquered, humiliated, and killed Arab people, dominated and exploited Arab countries, and tried to destroy the Islamic faith. And when President Bush described the war against terrorism as a "crusade," these Muslims felt threatened.

This crusade, this war on terrorism, is going to take awhile. And the American people must be patient.
PRESIDENT GEORGE W. BUSH[9]

Saddam Hussein intentionally draws parallels to history in what he says and does, not only referring to the Arab countries' recent humiliations, but going back hundreds and even thousands of years to make his point. For example, he called his war against Iran "Qadisiyat

Saddam," reminding the people of the battle against the Persians fought nearly 1,350 years ago!

A second example of Saddam Hussein's understanding of symbolism and history can be found in his efforts to rebuild Babylon. Moa'yad Saeed, director-general of the Iraqi Antiquities Department, described the rebuilding of Babylon as a symbol of the conflict between Iraq and Iran. "The Persians tried many times to overrun Iraq and they did it not only in Babylon. . . . They have been trying to do it for centuries."[10]

Echoing the same idea, the Iraqi Minister of Information and Culture, Latif Nsayyif Jassim, spoke at the opening of the Babylon International Festival. He compared the Iran-Iraq War, then in its seventh year, to the attack on Babylon by Cyrus in 539 B.C.: "We told Khomeini that Babylon will never be burnt twice. Today we tell him that Babylon at the time of President Saddam Hussein is recalling its past glories. It hosts this outstanding gathering of thinkers, educated people, and artists. It thus links ancient Babylon under Nebuchadnezzar and Hammurabi with the modern Babylon under President Saddam Hussein."[11]

When Babylon consisted of small city-states and separate dynasties, Hammurabi waged successive wars to unite these city-states so that Babylon remained as one city, as the bright light of civilization.

However, it suffered more and more from repeated attacks until Nebuchadnezzar came to power and reconstructed. He built temples and high walls as he realized it was the pulpit of the first Iraqi civilization.

Today looks exactly like yesterday.

After long periods of darkness that enveloped the land of Babylon and concealed its characteristics, Saddam Hussein emerges from Mesopotamia, as Hammurabi and Nebuchadnezzar had emerged, at a time to shake the century old dust off Babylon's face.

Saddam Hussein, the grandson of the Babylonians, the son of this great land, is leaving his fingerprints everywhere.

FROM NEBUCHADNEZZAR TO SADDAM HUSSEIN, BABYLON RISES AGAIN, booklet published by the Iraqis[12]

Saddam Hussein has compared himself to the warrior Saladin. He has traced his family tree back to the prophet Mohammed. But the person he compares himself to most often is Nebuchadnezzar.

13
The Grandson of the Babylonians

What is most important to me about Nebuchadnezzar is the link between the Arabs' abilities and the liberation of Palestine. Nebuchadnezzar was, after all, an Arab from Iraq, albeit ancient Iraq. Nebuchadnezzar was the one who brought the bound Jewish slaves from Palestine. That is why, whenever I remember Nebuchadnezzar, I like to remind the Arabs—Iraqis in particular—of their historical responsibilities. It is a burden that should not stop them from action, but rather spur them into action because of their history.

SADDAM HUSSEIN[1]

When asked if Hussein ever dreamed of filling a role such as that of Nebuchadnezzar or Saladin, an Arab hero who fought the Crusaders, Hussein replied, "By God, I do indeed dream and wish for this. It is an honor for any human being to dream of such a role."

DAVID LAMB in the *Los Angeles Times*[2]

Saddam Hussein first appeared on the scene as a pan-Arab politician. His great hero is Nebuchadnezzar II, who was neither an Arab or a Moslem, but the builder of a great empire (and the conqueror of Jerusalem).

WALTER LAQUEUR in the *Washington Post*[3]

Saddam Hussein has three ambitious goals:
territory, economic power, and the elimination of the
nation of Israel. Somehow it is not surprising that his
goals reflect the goals of Nebuchadnezzar, who also
wanted an empire, power, glory, and the destruction of
Jerusalem.

Like Nebuchadnezzar, Saddam Hussein is full of
pride.

Hussein . . . has used the arts and great artists not
for their own sake but as a tool to further his political goals and glorify himself. It is a mark of his
grip on society that he has co-opted so many
artists into going along, getting to live like million-
aires in exchange for their homages to him in
acrylic, steel, and literary verse. When the book is
written on Saddam Hussein, it will be said that
artists and poets were as vital to his reign as his
field commanders and his secret police.

CAROL MORELLO in the *Philadelphia Inquirer*[4]

Robed Bedouins, helmeted air force pilots and
women soldiers appear nightly on state television
in choirs to sing the praises of Hussein and the
valor of Iraq's fighting forces.

"Oh Saddam, our bullets sing to their clip
that they are always ready," croons the dapper
Yas Khuder as scenes of swooping jet fighters and
advancing tank battalions appear on the television
screen behind him.

San Jose Mercury News[5]

The tour guide at a reconstructed palace in Babylon described with enthusiasm the restored monuments of the ancient city—the lion sculpture, the brick reliefs of bulls and griffins, the newly planted hanging gardens. Then she got to the throne room and, with a sweep of her hand, she pointed to the empty platform. "This is where the leader Saddam Hussein had his throne. This is where Saddam Hussein sat," she said,

The short, stout woman looked around at the quizzical faces, then caught herself with a nervous laugh. "I mean Nebuchadnezzar. Nebuchadnezzar. Nebuchadnezzar had this throne here."

DANIEL WILLIAMS in the *Los Angeles Times*[6]

Hussein views Iraq as the continuation of Nebuchadnezzar's Babylon, and he wants to promote pan-Arab unity as the modern equivalent of Nebuchadnezzar's Babylonian Empire. He wishes to rule nothing less than a unified Arab nation that extends from Saudi Arabia in the south, through Syria and Jordan in the west, to Israel on the shores of the Mediterranean. Like Saladin, Saddam Hussein wants to lead the Arab armies in victory—to recapture Israel and drive the "infidels" from the West out of Arab lands.

The Tide Cannot Be Turned Back

I will endeavor to be one flame among many, no matter how bright I shine, and one sword among many, not the only sword.

SADDAM HUSSEIN[7]

Are these the dreams of a single deluded man? If military forces kill Hussein, will the conflict be ended?

No. Hussein has been able to articulate his vision and achieve his goals more completely than any Arab ruler in recent history, but he is not alone in his dream of a unified Arab nation. Nasser of Egypt reached for that goal in the fifties, and Hussein strives for it today. If Hussein disappears tomorrow from the international scene, someone else will pick up the battle cry. And there will be one more martyr to the cause of Arab unity.

During the twentieth century, scores of would-be conquerors have stalked the halls of power around the world. From Idi Amin in Uganda to Pol Pot in Cambodia to Nicolae Ceausescu in Romania, a parade of dictators has ruled by naked force and aggression. So why has the world vigorously responded to Saddam Hussein when it so often winks at the misdeeds of others? The answer is twofold: oil and weapons of mass destruction.

The machinery of the industrialized West runs on oil, and 50 percent of the world's oil reserves lie underground in the Middle East. Saddam Hussein's actions have the potential to affect the lives of everyone in the Western Hemisphere. Even more frightening is the realization that Hussein has devoted twenty years and billions of dollars to develop chemical, biological, and nuclear weapons of mass destruction.

But it wasn't until after the gulf war that U.N. inspectors uncovered Saddam's ambitious biological-weapons program. The inspectors destroyed

large stockpiles, and demolished key production
facilities. But they never believed they found
everything. And based on what the inspectors
found, Saddam could now be growing anthrax, *bot-
ulinum* toxin, and perhaps even smallpox strains.[8]

JOHN BARRY in *Newsweek*

In 1979, Khomeini came to power in Iran, threatening the stability of the Persian Gulf region. Khomeini's
anti-Western fervor threatened the lives of nations like
Saudi Arabia and Kuwait, which profit greatly from their
economic ties to Western countries. When Saddam Hussein went to war with Iran, he assumed the role of pro-
tector of the countries who did not have the military
might to oppose Iran.

But in the early days of 1990, Saddam Hussein was
broke. His country had just ended the costly war with
Iran, and he desperately needed to refill his nation's
coffers. Selling oil was the usual way to balance the
budget—but other Arab nations, including Kuwait, were
selling oil at less than twenty dollars a barrel.

If Kuwait had given him the money [Saddam]
demanded, the access to the Persian Gulf he
needed and the help he sought in pushing world oil
prices higher—Saddam would have settled for a
diplomatic solution between brotherly Arab states,
. . . [but] the Kuwaitis were stubborn. They were
ignoring his call for less oil production. Lower oil
prices were costing Iraq billions of dollars. From
Saddam Hussein's perspective, Kuwait's intransi-
gence was tantamount to economic warfare.

DAVID LAMB in the *Los Angeles Times*[9]

Saddam Hussein has always seemed nervous about territory. Part of the reason for beginning the war with Iran was to gain access to the Shatt al Arab waterway, indispensable to Iraq for exporting its oil. Kuwait, with its coastline and islands, offers free access to the Persian Gulf. Kuwait was also a small country, with a population of only two million and an army of only twenty thousand.[10]

At 2:00 A.M. on August 2, 1990, Soviet-made T-72 tanks of Iraq's Republican Guards swept over the desert and rumbled across Kuwait's border. Kuwait fell in less than six hours. Its emergency warning sirens never even sounded.[11]

Iraq's pre-invasion demands were clear: Hussein wanted full control of the Rumaila oil field it shared with Kuwait and possession of two Kuwaiti islands that hinder access to the Persian Gulf from the Iraqi port of Umm al Qasr. . . . When Arab leaders call for a summit, they are talking about such a deal. . . . The suggestion is that Hussein has a price—and it is the oil field and the islands.

NICK B. WILLIAMS, JR. in the *Los Angeles Times*[12]

Oil—and the money it provides—is a crucial key to the problem. As it does throughout the world, money talks in the Middle East—buying armies, economic aid, and allies. "If we can pay someone off and just produce enough oil, we'll be happy because we've got a lot to lose," said one member of the Saudi royal family.[13]

The Arab countries in many ways are like squabbling cousins in a large extended family. Though they are members of the same Arab "family," they are united only in their opposition to Israel.

> Against Israel, we will stand with Iraq.
> A Syrian government official[14]

> Believe me, no Arab will side with the Americans against the Iraqis. The majority of Arabs support Saddam. No other Arab leader has challenged the outside powers like Saddam. If I had the ability, yes, I would fight for him.
> **RIAD AASSI,** a Palestinian refugee in Jordan[15]

> For all their talk of brotherhood, Arabs do not trust Arabs. Nor do they depend on each other economically. Only 5 percent of Arab trade is interregional. Only 2 percent of the $140 billion Kuwait and Saudi Arabia have invested abroad is in Arab countries.
>
> But while the world moves toward a global society, the Arabs are backing away. They look not to Europe or to Japan or to Korea for models of successful development, because they fear that all outside influences will rob them of their "Arabness."
> **DAVID LAMB** in the *Los Angeles Times*[16]

Though Saudi Arabia and Kuwait helped finance the Iran-Iraq War, both countries are resented in the Arab world. Many Americans mistakenly assume that all Arabs are wealthy, but a great chasm separates the "haves" and the "have-nots" among the Arab people. Most of the Gulf states have relatively few people but tremendous oil reserves. The leaders live lavish lifestyles that include all the amenities of Western civilization.

In contrast, most of the more populous Arab countries are extremely poor. Many citizens of Egypt, Jordan, Lebanon, Syria, and Iraq live in abject poverty. Saddam Hussein has appealed to the anger and frustration of the "have-not" countries by claiming that the oil-rich countries have not shared their wealth equally with their Arab brothers.

Finally, for the first time since Egypt's Gamal Shawki Abdel Nasser, an Arab leader had been bold enough to stand up to the West and had said all the catchwords—Palestine, Islam, unity, sharing Arab oil—that reminded the Arabs how much should be right, and how much had gone wrong.

DAVID LAMB in the *Los Angeles Times*[17]

Strangely enough, Iraq sits on land with massive oil reserves. Hasim F. Al-Khersan, director-general of the Oil Exploration Company, states that only 104 exploratory wells have been drilled in Iraq over the past twenty years, and 95 percent of the drilling activity was east of the Tigris River. "We think what we have discovered is less than half of the oil potential [of Iraq]."[18]

Iraq contains one of the planet's largest reserves [of oil]. President George W. Bush would hardly go after Saddam for the oil alone, but it's certainly a factor.

JANE BRYANT QUINN in *Newsweek*[19]

The reason Iraq is among the "have-not" countries is that much of Iraq's oil wealth has gone into purchasing military hardware and constructing monuments. Between 1983 and 1988, Iraq spent $34 billion to outfit and modernize Saddam Hussein's army. And since the Gulf War, sanctions placed on Iraq have limited the amount of oil it is allowed to sell on the open market.

With the largest army in the Arab world, Saddam Hussein set out in 1990 to forge a worldwide economic empire, its boundaries established by Nebuchadnezzar over twenty-five-hundred years ago. The West built a powerful coalition to thwart Hussein's plans. The Iraqi army was defeated, but it was not completely destroyed. Hussein's ambitions were checked, but he remained in power. Kuwait was liberated, but Saddam's goals remain unaltered. And the economic prize he still seeks is control of half the world's oil supply.

Saddam Hussein has held numerous meetings with Iraqi nuclear scientists, a group he calls his "nuclear mujahideen"—his nuclear holy warriors. . . .

If the Iraqi regime is able to produce, buy, or steal an amount of highly enriched uranium a little larger than a single softball, it could have a nuclear weapon in less than a year. And if we allow that to happen, a terrible line would be crossed. Saddam Hussein would be in a position to blackmail anyone who opposes his aggression. He would be in a position to dominate the Middle East.

PRESIDENT GEORGE W. BUSH[20]

If Saddam Hussein gains that control, he will gain untold wealth. In addition, he will gain power over a region of the world that desperately craves redress for past grievances. Like Nebuchadnezzar, he will be ruler of the Middle East—and beyond.

14
Babylon Today: A City in Waiting

While Mr. Hussein struggles with the crisis caused
by his invasion of Kuwait, the Iraqi leader's construction plans appear to have been shelved. A
huge new palace that some Iraqis suspect was to
have been Mr. Hussein's is abandoned while only
half-built, standing like a sentinel above King Nebuchadnezzar's ruins. Instead of the Hanging Gardens, which long since crumbled into dust, there
is an artificial lake fringed with fast-food restau-
rants, and they too are shut down.

JOHN BURNS in the *New York Times International*[1]

The situation unfolding in the Middle East as
I write is reminiscent of the ancient battles pitting Babylon intermittently against Egypt, Assyria, Judah, and
Persia. Everything old is news again, and the descendants of men who fought each other thousands of years
ago are still threatening war in the hot desert sands of
the Middle East.

One thing is certain: Babylon, the great city of man,
is waiting. She will rise again to become a great power,
a seat of trade and religion. Just as she played a leading
role at the beginning of time, so she will be a leading
lady in the last days.

I, Nebuchadnezzar, King of Babylon,
I am the son of Nabopolassar, King of Babylon.
I who erected the Ezida Temple,
I who built Procession Street,
The Street of the Forgiven Son,
The Street of Nebu,
And paved it with shimmering stones.
Nebu, you the divine minister,
Grant me immortality.

BABYLONIAN INSCRIPTION[2]

15
Babylon's Fall Foretold

The prophet Isaiah preached during dark days in Judah's history. Over a hundred years before Nebuchadnezzar's reign, Isaiah predicted Judah's fall to Babylon. But this was not all Isaiah had to say about Babylon. In chapters 13 and 14, Isaiah penned a series of stunning predictions about the city of man.

A century after Isaiah died, the prophet Jeremiah walked through the streets of Jerusalem with his message of judgment and blessing. During his ministry, Babylon was at the zenith of its power, but remarkably, Jeremiah joined Isaiah in predicting Babylon's future. The words of both prophets read like the headlines of today's newspapers.

The Prophets Indict the Nations

The early chapters of Isaiah are concerned with God's judgment on the nation of Judah. Beginning in chapter 13, however, Isaiah looks at the surrounding Gentile nations and says to them, "If God will judge His own people for their sins, what makes you think you can escape?" Isaiah then names twelve other cities or nations in a "hall of shame": Babylon, Assyria, Philistia, Moab, Israel, Damascus, Cush, Egypt, Babylon, Edom, Arabia, Jerusalem, and Tyre.

Isaiah gives Babylon special emphasis. He lists it first, he lists it twice, and he spends more time writing about Babylon's judgment than any other nation's.

Most events prophesied in the book of Isaiah came true during the prophet's lifetime. His second set of prophecies about Babylon (Isaiah 21:1–10) were fulfilled around 700 B.C. But the events concerning Babylon described in the thirteenth and fourteenth chapters of Isaiah were not fulfilled in Isaiah's lifetime. They have never been fulfilled.

Jeremiah also made predictions about the Gentile nations surrounding Judah (Jeremiah 46:1–51:64). His "hit list" began with Egypt, the nation that had enticed Judah to rebel against Babylon and then backed out of a promise to support the Jews. Jeremiah then announced God's judgment upon Judah's neighbors: the Philistines, Moab, Ammon, Edom, and Damascus (Syria). Finally, Jeremiah announced judgment on three groups of nations to the distant east: Kedar and Hazor in the Arabian peninsula, Elam in modern-day Iran, and Babylon.

Jeremiah did not place Babylon last on his list by accident. Instead, he built to a climax, listing Babylon last to emphasize the city's punishment.

Babylon's Judgment Is Still Future

What did Isaiah predict for Babylon, the mighty city? First, Babylon will be destroyed at "the day of the LORD."

> *Wail, for the day of the LORD is near; it will come like destruction from the Almighty. . . . See, the day of the LORD is coming—a cruel day, with wrath and fierce anger—to make the land desolate and destroy the sinners within it.*
>   ISAIAH 13:6, 9

In the Old Testament, "the day of the LORD" originally referred to any time God entered history to settle accounts with humankind. However, the phrase soon came to refer to a special day of judgment and blessing that would come on the entire earth.

The prophet Joel described the Day of the Lord as a time when "the earth shakes, the sky trembles, the sun and moon are darkened, and the stars no longer shine" (Joel 2:10). The prophet Malachi closed the Old Testament by promising that God would "send you the prophet Elijah before that great and dreadful day of the LORD comes" (Malachi 4:5).

As the concept of the Day of the Lord developed in the Bible, it came to refer to the unique period of judgment coming on all the world but especially the nation of Israel. Daniel described it as "a time of distress such as has not happened from the beginning of nations until then" (Daniel 12:1).

Jesus described it even more clearly: "For then there will be great distress, unequaled from the beginning of the world until now—and never to be equaled again. If those days had not been cut short, no one would survive" (Matthew 24:21–22).

In Isaiah 13 the prophet predicts that Babylon will exist and will be destroyed in the day of the Lord. God will unleash supernatural judgments in the heavens and on the earth. "The stars of heaven and their constellations will not show their light. The rising sun will be darkened and the moon will not give its light. . . . Therefore I will make the heavens tremble; and the earth will shake from its place at the wrath of the LORD Almighty, in the day of his burning anger" (Isaiah 13:10, 13).

The book of Revelation describes further supernatural judgments that will be poured out on the earth during this coming period of divine judgment on Babylon: earthquakes and cosmic disturbances, thunder and lightning, pollution, hailstorms.[1]

Isaiah provides one additional clue that lets us know he is talking about the final annihilation of Babylon in the last days, not some temporary razing. God declares that He will destroy Babylon when He "will punish the world for its evil, the wicked for their sins" (Isaiah 13:11). From shortly after the time of the Flood, Babylon has symbolized humanity's rebellion against God. When God destroys Babylon, He will destroy all the evil in the world.

Babylon Will Be Destroyed by Many Nations

If Babylon will be destroyed in the end times, who will destroy it? The United States? Will Americans wipe out Iraq? Unfortunately, Isaiah does not give us any information specifically about the United States. But the United States is a major world power—how could it *not* play a major role in the last days?

The Bible predicts a seven-year period of prophetic history before the second coming of Jesus Christ to the earth. God's prophetic clock will begin ticking when a world ruler, called in various places the prince, the Antichrist, or the Beast, makes a seven-year treaty with the nation of Israel (Daniel 9:27). In some way this treaty will seem to guarantee Israel's peace and safety and will provide an apparent solution to the Arab-Israeli conflict in the Middle East.

This leader will arise from the remnants of the Roman Empire, probably Europe or the area of the Mediterranean basin. He will control an empire of ten nations and will dominate the world through military power.[2] But the peace with Israel will be shattered midway through the seven years. The leader will arrive in Israel, enter the temple (which will have been rebuilt by the Jews), and declare himself to be God.[3] A statue of this man will be erected in the temple, and everyone will be ordered to bow down to the image.[4]

The construction of the statue marks a turning point. For the first three and a half years Israel will enjoy a state of relative peace, protected by her treaty with this world ruler. But for the final three and a half years, this false messiah will turn his worldwide empire against the Jewish people. Unleashing a hatred even worse than Hitler's, the Antichrist will devote his energies to eradicating God's people.[5] He will not be stopped until Christ returns to earth to rescue His people and reestablish His rule over the nations.[6]

America Is Strangely Absent

So where does the United States fit into the picture? It is clear from Scripture that the dominant political and military power will center around the Mediterranean and Europe—not the United States. By the end times, the United States will no longer be a major influence in the world. But how can this be, especially since we are playing such a major role in the Middle East today?

First, it is possible that the United States is not mentioned in prophecy because we will become a second-class international power overnight when God removes Christians from the earth, an event scheduled to occur just before the beginning of this seven-year period. True believers who have placed their faith in Jesus Christ will be taken to heaven before the Antichrist is revealed.[7]

Today as many as half of all Americans claim to be "born again," or believers in Jesus Christ. If only one-fourth of that number have genuinely made a personal commitment to Christ, then over 28 million Americans will suddenly "disappear" when God removes His church from the earth![8]

Can you imagine the effects on our country if over 28 million people—people in industry, government, the military, business, agriculture, education, medicine, and communications—disappear? That is approximately double the entire population of New York City, Los Angeles, Chicago, and Houston all rolled together!

The economic turmoil that followed the horrific attacks on the World Trade Center and the Pentagon will pale in comparison to the political and economic collapse that will occur when our society suddenly loses individuals who were its "salt and light." America could not support an army in the Middle East because the military would be needed at home to control the chaos!

Second, it is possible that America could become a second-class society *before* the church is taken from the earth. Our country is now undergoing a time of unprecedented secularization. In the past, God has blessed America because it provided the ideal soil for His Word to take root and flourish. Our founding principles included freedom of religion, and religious revivals swept through the country during the nineteenth century. Missionaries from the United States took the good news of salvation through Jesus Christ into the remotest parts of the world, and with that good news came advances in agriculture, medicine, government, and morality.

But today America is declining morally. Our quest for freedom has come to center on the freedom to rip away our moral underpinnings and trample on our religious heritage. When a country ceases to produce fruits of righteousness, it can no longer expect God to bless.

Further, God has blessed America because of America's friendship with the Jewish people and the state of Israel. When God called Abraham, He promised that

He would "bless those who bless you, and whoever curses you I will curse" (Genesis 12:3). That principle still holds today. Though the United States has not always treated the Jews as well as it should, this country still has been a haven of refuge for Jews fleeing persecution in other countries.

The United States was the first country to recognize the state of Israel, and we have been Israel's close ally and supporter for the past five decades. In recent years, however, our support for Israel has been waning. Some have even mistakenly blamed our friendship with Israel for the terrorist attacks against our country.

The minute the United States turns its back on the state of Israel, we have made ourselves an enemy of God. This does not mean we must condone everything Israel does, but we must never cease to affirm the right for Israel to exist as a nation in the land God has promised her.

A third possible explanation of why the United States is not pictured in the end times is more sinister. If terrorists ever find a way to unleash chemical, biological, or nuclear weapons in our cities, the resulting chaos could force us into a period of decline. Before September 11, 2001, such a thought seemed highly unlikely. But now it is much easier to imagine how our nation could be frightened into abdicating our leading role on the stage of world events.

Fourth, perhaps we will suffer a military defeat or simply weaken in our national resolve. Financial crises at home could increase our isolationist tendencies.

After Vietnam, few Americans wanted to become involved in a war that would require us to pay a price in physical resources or human lives. We are an "instant" society, and we want our wars to be short-lived, nearly bloodless affairs like Grenada, Panama, or the Gulf War. But when the loss of American lives mounts, as it did in Somalia, America has struggled to maintain the course. We balk at the idea of a protracted war requiring a heavy commitment in money and lives.

But anything less than victory in the current struggles against the twin threats of terrorism and Saddam Hussein will further weaken America's resolve and could force us to abdicate our role as a world leader.

16
The Time of the Lord's Vengeance

If the United States is not the dominant power in prophetic end-time events, who is? Isaiah identifies two distinct groups of nations that will gather for war against Babylon. The first group is not specifically identified, but Isaiah describes its composition:

> Listen, a noise on the mountains, like that of a great multitude! Listen, an uproar among the kingdoms, like nations massing together! The LORD Almighty is mustering an army for war. They come from faraway lands, from the ends of the heavens—the LORD and the weapons of his wrath—to destroy the whole country.
>
> ISAIAH 13:4–5

The army massing against Babylon is a great multitude from many nations, not from the Gulf area, but from faraway lands. This multinational force will destroy not only Babylon, but the whole country.

Writing almost a hundred years after Isaiah, Jeremiah predicts the arrival of the same international force.

> *"For I will stir up and bring against Babylon an alliance of great nations from the land of the north. . . . Look! An army is coming from the north; a great nation and many kings are being stirred up from the ends of the earth. They are armed with bows and spears; they are cruel and without mercy. They sound like the roaring sea as they ride on their horses; they come like men in battle formation to attack you, O Daughter of Babylon."*
> JEREMIAH 50:9, 41–42

When the multinational force marches upon Babylon, it will approach not from the southern direction of the Arabian peninsula, but from the north. Advancing through Turkey, Syria, or Jordan, the mighty army will move from north to south against the city of Babylon.

A second group will also come against the Babylonians. This group is identified in Isaiah 13:17 as "the Medes." This army will annihilate the people of Babylon:

> *Whoever is captured will be thrust through; all who are caught will fall by the sword. Their infants will be dashed to pieces before their eyes; their houses will be looted and their wives ravished. . . . Their bows will strike down the young*

men; they will have no mercy on infants nor will they look with compassion on children.
ISAIAH 13:15–16, 18

Jeremiah confirms that the Medes will be part of the group to attack Babylon (Jeremiah 51:11, 28). Who are these Medes?

Some think that Isaiah was referring to Cyrus and the Persians who occupied Babylon in 539 B.C., but Cyrus entered the city without a battle and with little bloodshed. So who are the Medes who will come and take no prisoners?

The Medes were a people who occupied the mountainous area of northwestern Iran and northeastern Iraq. This is the area occupied by the Kurdish people today. They have been fighting Turkey, Iran, and Iraq in an attempt to establish their own independent country of Kurdistan. Saddam Hussein killed thousands of their women and children in 1987 and 1988 with poison gas. Following the Gulf War, the United States encouraged the Kurds to oppose Saddam Hussein. Unfortunately, that revolt was brutally crushed by the Iraqi army. The hatred of the Kurdish people toward the government of Iraq parallels the hatred of the Medes for the Babylonians described by the prophet Isaiah. The Kurds will take their revenge on the women and children of Babylon.

Babylon Will Be Suddenly Destroyed

Babylon, the city that wanted to stand forever, will collapse quickly under the harsh hand of God's judgment. God compares Himself to a lion pouncing suddenly on an unsuspecting foe: "Like a lion coming up from Jordan's thickets to a rich pastureland, I will chase Babylon from its land in an instant" (Jeremiah 50:44).

Jeremiah compares Babylon's collapse to someone suffering a sudden illness: "Babylon will suddenly fall and be broken. Wail over her! Get balm for her pain; perhaps she can be healed." But, quickly closing the door on this possibility, Jeremiah then announces: "She cannot be healed" (Jeremiah 51:8–9). Babylon's sudden illness will be fatal.

Babylon's great and sudden devastation will not come from a natural disaster. No earthquake, fire, or flood will be her undoing. Babylon will fall suddenly in battle.

> *"One courier follows another and messenger follows messenger to announce to the king of Babylon that his entire city is captured."*
> JEREMIAH 51:31

One messenger after another will rush in and announce to the ruler of Babylon that the city is surrounded on all sides. Babylon will fall suddenly and completely.

Babylon Will Never Be Reinhabited

> *Babylon, the jewel of kingdoms, the glory of the Babylonians' pride, will be overthrown by God like Sodom and Gomorrah.*
> ISAIAH 13:19

In my many travels to Israel, I have taken over five thousand slides and pictures, but I have yet to get a picture of Sodom or Gomorrah. When God destroyed these cities in the time of Abraham, He "rained down burning sulfur on Sodom and Gomorrah" (Genesis 19:24). These cities were covered with burning sulfur and then submerged beneath what is now the southern end of the Dead Sea. From the moment God overthrew them, these cities ceased to exist and were never again inhabited as cities.

Isaiah predicted that Babylon's destruction will parallel that of Sodom and Gomorrah. Throughout the centuries, Babylon has been captured or had parts of its walls torn down, but it has never been completely destroyed.

Jeremiah predicted that Babylon's towers will fall and her walls will be torn down. The dwellings will be set on fire, and the bars of her gates will be broken (Jeremiah 50:15; 51:30). These prophecies were not fulfilled when Cyrus captured Babylon in 539 B.C. Babylon the Great has never been completely demolished and razed.

> *[Babylon] will never be inhabited or lived in through all generations; no Arab will pitch his tent there, no shepherd will rest his flocks there.*
> ISAIAH 13:20

Isaiah further added that Babylon "will never be inhabited or lived in through all generations." Cities were occasionally abandoned for short periods of time due to war, plague, or famine, but virtually all cities were reinhabited when danger had passed. But once Babylon falls, it will never be inhabited again—not by anyone, not for any length of time.

Jeremiah also predicted the complete desolation of Babylon. Not only will the city be uninhabited, but "her towns will be desolate, a dry and desert land, a land where no one lives, through which no man travels" (Jeremiah 51:43). The life-giving waters of the Euphrates River will dry up, and the land of Iraq will be turned into a bleak and barren wilderness. The land will become totally uninhabitable.

Babylon's Useless Bricks

When Robert Koldewey first came to Babylon at the end of the nineteenth century, he found entire sections of the city being mined for bricks. "The astonishing deep pits and galleries that occur in places owe their origin to the quarrying for brick that has been carried on extensively during the last decades. The buildings of ancient Babylon, with their excellent kiln bricks, served even in antiquity, perhaps in Roman times, certainly in Parthian days, as a quarry for common use."[1]

Babylon's fine bricks have been in use for centuries, but after her complete and final destruction, Jeremiah writes, "No rock will be taken from you for a cornerstone, nor any stone for a foundation, for you will be desolate forever" (Jeremiah 51:26). Babylon will not even survive as part of another city. Not one brick will ever be used again.

God's People Must Flee from Babylon

Because Babylon will suffer a bloody defeat, Jeremiah calls on anyone who wishes to save his or her life to escape from Babylon: "Flee from Babylon! Run for your lives!" (Jeremiah 51:6).

The prophet Daniel lived in Babylon on the very night the city fell to Cyrus, and he was studying Jeremiah's prophecies (Daniel 9:1–2). Since Daniel did not flee that night, it seems likely that he understood this was not the night of Babylon's total and bloody eradication. But when that time does come, all who can read and understand God's Word should flee from Babylon and Iraq as quickly as possible.

The Motivation for Destruction

Why will Babylon be judged? God announces Babylon's fall because of her sin against God's people and her destruction of God's temple. But those who destroy Babylon do not know they are acting as God's agents. They are coming to plunder Babylon, to strip away her wealth. Whatever Babylon has, whether it is oil or some other form of wealth, other nations will desire and seize it.

God Restores Israel

After God destroys Babylon, Jeremiah tells us what will happen when the nation of Israel gathers again:

"In those days, at that time," declares the LORD, "the people

*of Israel and the people of Judah together will go in tears to
seek the LORD their God. They will ask the way to Zion and
turn their faces toward it. They will come and bind themselves to the LORD in an everlasting covenant that will not be
forgotten."*

JEREMIAH 50:4–5

Following the death of King Solomon, the Israelites
had divided into two separate nations. The northern
kingdom, called Israel, broke away from the descendants of David, set up a false religious system, chose
kings who were unrighteous, and remained an independent country until it was destroyed as a nation in
722 B.C. by the Assyrians.

The southern kingdom, Judah, continued to keep
its capital in Jerusalem and was ruled by a descendant
of David until the nation was conquered and destroyed
by the Babylonians.

After Babylon's destruction, both nations will return
to the Land of Promise. God will make a new covenant
with them,[2] a covenant that will be written "on their
hearts," so that they will have both a knowledge of God's
righteous standards and the internal ability to keep those
standards (Jeremiah 31:33).

This new covenant will make it possible for their
wickedness to be forgiven. How? By providing a substitute who paid the penalty for mankind's sin. The new
covenant promised by Jeremiah was inaugurated at the
death of Jesus Christ on the cross.

Isaiah predicted what will happen next to Israel:

The LORD will have compassion on Jacob; once again he will choose Israel and will settle them in their own land. Aliens will join them and unite with the house of Jacob. Nations will take them and bring them to their own place. And the house of Israel will possess the nations as menservants and maidservants in the LORD's land. They will make captives of their captors and rule over their oppressors.

ISAIAH 14:1–2

This restoration predicted by Isaiah did not occur when a remnant of Jews returned to the land following the fall of Babylon to Cyrus in 539 B.C., nor was it fulfilled when Israel returned to the land in 1948. At neither time was Israel brought back to the land by Gentiles who pledged allegiance to Israel and allowed Israel to rule over them.

What Isaiah was describing is the still-future regathering of the nation of Israel that will occur when Jesus Christ returns to earth to set up His messianic kingdom. God will bring the nations of Israel and Judah back to the Promised Land and allow them to enjoy the benefits of the new covenant that began with the death of Christ. The nation will experience the indwelling presence of the Holy Spirit and know full and complete forgiveness of sin.

"In those days, at that time," declares the LORD, "search will be made for Israel's guilt, but there will be none, and for the sins of Judah, but none will be found, for I will forgive the remnant I spare."

JEREMIAH 50:20

> *"And I will pour out on the house of David and the inhabi-*
> *tants of Jerusalem a spirit of grace and supplication. They*
> *will look on me, the one they have pierced, and they will*
> *mourn for him as one mourns for an only child, and grieve*
> *bitterly for him as one grieves for a firstborn son. . . . On that*
> *day a fountain will be opened to the house of David and the*
> *inhabitants of Jerusalem, to cleanse them from sin and impu-*
> *rity."*
> ZECHARIAH 12:10; 13:1

Israel and Judah will experience forgiveness of sin when they see Jesus Christ returning to earth at His second coming. They will realize that He is their Messiah and that He died for their sins, and they will turn to Him as their Savior.

The judgment of Babylon will serve as a catalyst that will culminate other end-time events and lead to the restoration of Israel and the establishment of Christ's rule from Israel over the entire world.

Throughout history, Babylon has represented the height of rebellion and opposition to God's plans and purposes, so God allows Babylon to continue during the final days. It is almost as though He "calls her out" for a final duel. But this time, the conflict between God and Babylon ends decisively. The city of Babylon will be destroyed, and the city of Jerusalem will be restored in an everlasting covenant of forgiveness.

17
Babylon in the Book of Revelation

The book of Revelation, with all of its apocalyptic visions of beasts, bowls, and brimstone, frightens and confuses most readers. Is it a hopeless maze of disconnected visions, or is it prophecy that we can understand? And what does Revelation have to say about what will happen in our future?

From the first chapter to the last, Revelation claims to be a prophecy of future events:

> *The revelation of Jesus Christ, which God gave him to show his servants what must soon take place. . . . "Do not seal up*

the words of the prophecy of this book, because the time is near. . . . Behold, I am coming soon!"
REVELATION 1:1; 22:10, 12

Written by the apostle John, the first chapters of Revelation are composed of seven letters to seven different churches. But beginning in Revelation 4:1 Christ tells John: "Come up here, and I will show you what must take place after this." The remainder of the book of Revelation focuses on events that are still future, and chapters 6 through 21 picture a time when God's program once again revolves around the nation of Israel.

In the future, the witness to God will come from "all the tribes of Israel."[1] The world's focus will center on a Jewish temple that will be rebuilt in the city of Jerusalem,[2] and prophets patterned after Moses and Elijah will rise once again in God's city.[3] Satan will persecute the nation of Israel (the "woman clothed with the sun, with the moon under her feet and a crown of twelve stars"[4]), and the gathering for the final battle of the ages will take place at Armageddon—the hill of Megiddo that guards the Jezreel Valley in northern Israel.

John Walvoord, chancellor of Dallas Theological Seminary, said preachers were laughed at 50 years ago when they quoted the Bible as placing the great final battle in the Middle East.

"Skeptics laughed because the Middle East was insignificant and could never be the center of action," Walvoord said. "Now, for the first time, people believe the power that is in the Middle East. They're not laughing today."

MICHAEL HIRSLEY AND JORGE CASUSO in the *Chicago Tribune*[5]

Old Testament Images

The language and imagery of Revelation comes from the Old Testament. As Ferrell Jenkins noted, "The book of Revelation is the most thoroughly Jewish in its language and imagery of any New Testament book. The book speaks not the language of Paul, but of the Old Testament prophets Isaiah, Ezekiel, and Daniel."[6]

If the Old Testament prophecies are like pieces of a large jigsaw puzzle, then Revelation is the completed picture on the top of the box that illustrates how the pieces come together. Prophecies about the time of trouble, the second coming of Christ, the destruction of Babylon, the restoration of Israel, and God's creation of a new heaven and earth are all found in the Old Testament. Revelation ties these prophecies together.

Chapters 6 through 19 explain what will take place on earth during the seven-year period of tribulation. John fits the pieces of God's future plan into a seven-year period first mentioned in Daniel 9:27:

> *"He will confirm a covenant with many for one 'seven.' In the middle of the 'seven' he will put an end to sacrifice and offering. And on a wing of the temple he will set up an abomination that causes desolation, until the end that is decreed is poured out on him."*

Daniel's Seventy Weeks

In Daniel 9, God gave a prophetic timetable for the nation of Israel. The clock began ticking when the command went out to restore and rebuild Jerusalem following its destruction by Babylon.[7] Israel's timetable was divided into seventy groups of seven years, a total of 490 years.

The first sixty-nine groups of years, or 483 years, counted the years "from the issuing of the decree to restore and rebuild Jerusalem until the Anointed One, the ruler, comes" (Daniel 9:25). The "Anointed One" is the Hebrew word for Messiah and refers to Jesus Christ. The day Christ rode into Jerusalem to proclaim Himself Israel's Messiah[8] was exactly 483 years to the day after the command to restore and rebuild Jerusalem had been given.[9]

God's prophetic clock stopped at that point. Daniel describes a gap between these 483 years and the final seven years of Israel's prophetic timetable. Several events will take place during this "gap."

First, the Anointed One will be killed.

Second, the "people of the ruler who will come will destroy the city and the sanctuary" (Daniel 9:26).

The "ruler who will come" is the still-future false messiah, or Antichrist; and his people, the Romans, fulfilled this prophecy when they destroyed both the city of Jerusalem and the temple in A.D. 70.

The third event that will take place in this gap is described as a time of difficulty and hardship for the Jews: "War will continue until the end, and desolations have been decreed." From A.D. 70 until today, the Jewish people have experienced times of great difficulty, sadness, and hardship.

The final "week" of seven years will begin for Israel when the Antichrist will confirm a covenant for seven years. A pact, or peace treaty, will be made with the nation of Israel, and this agreement will start the clock ticking on the final seven-year period in Israel's time of trouble. Israel will believe she has finally achieved peace because of the protection offered by this mighty world ruler, but in the middle of the seven years, the false messiah will "put an end to sacrifice and offering. And on a wing of the temple he will set up an abomination" (Daniel 9:27).

The False Messiah Brings Trouble on Israel

The final three-and-a-half years of this period are a time of unparalleled trouble for the nation of Israel. Jesus Christ described this "abomination that causes desolation" (Matthew 24:15) and indicated that its fulfillment was still in the future.

When this statue or image is finally set up in the temple, "then let those who are in Judea flee to the mountains. . . . For then there will be great distress, unequaled from the beginning of the world until now —and never to be equaled again" (Matthew 24:16, 21).

John describes these same events in Revelation 13. He pictures this future world ruler as a "beast" who will be empowered by Satan and who will persecute the Jews for "forty-two months," or three-and-a-half years, the same amount of time predicted by Daniel (Revelation 13:5).

John explains the "abomination that causes desolation" spoken of by Daniel and by Christ. The abomination will be an image of the Beast that will be set up in the temple in Jerusalem.

> *He ordered them to set up an image in honor of the beast who*
> *was wounded by the sword and yet lived. He was given*
> *power to give breath to the image of the first beast, so that it*
> *could speak and cause all who refused to worship the image*
> *to be killed.*
>
> REVELATION 13:14–15

All who refuse to worship this statue are executed. This seven-year period ends with the second coming of Jesus Christ to earth to judge sin and set up His kingdom over the entire earth (Revelation 19:11–21).

Sounds familiar, doesn't it? Just as Nebuchadnezzar put his statue out on the plain of Dura and tested the loyalty of his subjects, including Zedekiah, king of Judah, so will this future Antichrist erect some sort of statue or image and demand that people pay homage to it. The penalty for refusal? Death!

Seven Years of Judgment

In chapters 6 through 19 of the book of Revelation, John provides us with a chronological map to guide us through the seven-year time of trouble. The seal, trumpet, and bowl judgments unfold in sequence, with the final seven bowl judgments occurring at the end of the age. The period ends with a last gasp of grief as lightning, thunder, earthquakes, and a hailstorm mark the time of transition between the period of judgment and the return of Christ.

John digresses from his "calendar of events" to describe other activities that will occur during this period.

He gives information about flourishing worldwide missionary activity in this time (chapter 7), the supernatural struggle between angelic and demonic forces that persecute Israel (chapter 12), the character and activities of the evil world ruler (chapter 13), and God's destruction of Babylon (chapters 17–18).

Two Starring Roles in the Final Drama

Babylon plays a significant role in the end-time activities. If we read only the prophecies of Isaiah, Jeremiah, and Zechariah, we might conclude that the major end-time evil empire would be centered in the Middle East, in the country of Iraq, in the city of Babylon.

But Daniel painted a different picture of the end times. In both Nebuchadnezzar's and Daniel's dreams, God showed that a series of four world empires would dominate the times of the Gentiles: Babylon, Medo-Persia, Greece, and Rome. Each would rise and exert control over the city of Jerusalem. The fourth empire will be in existence when God reestablishes His kingdom over Israel.

When Christ came to earth and offered the kingdom to Israel,[10] the Gentile power then in control was Rome. Because the people of Israel rejected Christ as their Messiah, God's kingdom plan was suspended. God wasn't surprised that His nation rejected their Messiah. In fact, Daniel had predicted that the Messiah would be "cut off" (Daniel 9:26).

The Roman Beast and His Leading Lady

The world ruler who will arise during the final seven-year period will originate from somewhere within the territory occupied by the ancient Roman Empire. He will lead a new "revived" Roman Empire that will become the dominant power in the world.

The Roman Empire controlled much of the Mediterranean basin and Europe. This is the region from which the Antichrist will arise, and this is the region that will become the dominant military power during the tribulation period. But Europe? What European country is stronger than the United States?

Recent events have shown how rapidly the world can change. The entire political landscape of Europe was altered when, after forty years of division and tension, the Iron Curtain fell. Plans for a united Europe are now well under way. The euro has been adopted as the unifying currency. It is easy to imagine a ruler emerging who will unite Europe into a dominant military power stronger than any the world has ever known. This is the final empire predicted by Daniel.

But how can two end-time powers exist? How can we have a revived Roman Empire and a rebuilt Babylon that will also dominate the world?

In Revelation 17, John describes a vision with two parts. The first part of the vision is a woman identified as "Babylon." She is a city of extreme wealth that controls "peoples, multitudes, nations and languages" (Revelation 17:5, 15). She is the literal rebuilt city of Babylon.

The second part of John's vision is a "beast" that

describes both an individual and the empire he rules. He is a man who is given "power and his throne and great authority" by Satan (Revelation 13:2). He exerts military control over the earth for "forty-two months" as everyone else on the earth exclaims, "Who is like the beast? Who can make war against him?" (Revelation 13:4–5).

This beast has "ten horns" and "a mouth to utter proud words" that identify him as the fourth Gentile empire described in Daniel's dream (Daniel 7:7–8, 23–25). He is a world military ruler who comes from the revived Roman, or European, Empire.

Two world powers will arise in the end times. Babylon will predominantly be an economic power known for her vast wealth. The revived Roman Empire will be predominantly a military power. And yet, according to John's vision, Babylon will control the Antichrist during the tribulation period.

How could that be? How can a city control the world's mightiest army? Very easily. Consider present-day Saudi Arabia and the United States. The United States is the dominant military power. In fact, when Saddam Hussein threatened Saudi Arabia's borders, the Saudis called on America for help.

On the other hand, in the 1970s when Saudi Arabia turned off its oil supply, which nation sat in lines waiting to buy gasoline? We did! And in late 2000–2001, when Saudi Arabia cut back on its oil production in support of the Palestinian *Intifada,* who saw the price of gasoline climb to unbearably high levels? Again, we did! Americans are dependent upon Saudi oil reserves, and the actions of Saudi Arabia affect the United States.

We might be in the opening phase of a permanent oil war, pitting buyers, such as the United States, against the major sellers (and their allies) in the Middle East.

JANE BRYANT QUINN in *Newsweek*[11]

The country that controls the oil controls the destiny of an oil-dependent world.

18
The Scene Is Set

These prophecies of the Bible will be fulfilled. The only part in question is *when* God will bring them to pass. But even today a person of discernment can watch as the various players audition for their roles and the necessary scenes move into place. Babylon rises from her sleep; Europe is uniting; the United States is struggling economically and declining morally.

Consider this carefully: If the church left the world tomorrow, the United States would collapse as a world power. Russia continues to struggle economically. Japan and the rest of Asia have great potential, but they are still not strong militarily. Only the emerging European nations have the capability to replace the United States as an effective international military force in the coming days.

But Europe is *heavily* dependent on Middle Eastern oil. If Iraq could gain control of the oil resources of Saudi Arabia and the other Gulf states, perhaps in an Arab union, it could control Europe—and the world—economically.

Jabra, a Palestinian who has lived in Iraq for 40 years, sees Iraq's conquest of Kuwait not as the act of a bully but as the end result of "rising political consciousness, with an understanding of history as different from what the British and Western histories taught us about this area, and a feeling that we can reconsider these political boundaries."

Jabra looks down the telescope of history and sees a "tide of Arab nationalism that will sweep away the barefooted sheiks and semiliterate feudal lords" of the Arabian Peninsula.

"Arabs are one nationality that has the right to live within one state, free to determine its own destiny," according to the Baath Party constitution.

JOHN YEMMA in the *Boston Globe*[1]

Almost two thousand years ago, the apostle John predicted that two major world powers would rise in the end times. The woman, Babylon, will gain tremendous wealth and exert economic control over the world. The Beast, a revived Roman Empire, will become the dominant military power in the region but will depend on Babylon for oil. The Beast has the military might to destroy Babylon if he desires. For most of the tribulation period, however, he chooses not to because he needs her oil.

Finally, though, the Antichrist and his allies march on Babylon, fulfilling the prophecies of Isaiah and Jeremiah. They come from the north, almost at the end of the seven-year time of trouble. The last bowl of God's judgment, reserved for the end of the tribulation period, pours out upon Babylon, and she is destroyed.

The Meaning of "Babylon"

All of the seventeenth and eighteenth chapters of Revelation are devoted to Babylon's fall, and a heavenly hallelujah chorus joyfully rings after Babylon's defeat (Revelation 19:1–3). But is John referring to Babylon, the physical city, or a composite of various political and religious powers?

Many Bible teachers have long believed that there are two distinct Babylons described in Revelation 17 and 18: one, a "religious" Babylon that will be destroyed by the Antichrist in the middle of the tribulation period, and another, an "economic" Babylon, the Antichrist's capital city that will be destroyed at the end of the tribulation period.

But I am convinced that the Babylon John is describing is the Babylon whose end-time existence and subsequent annihilation were predicted by the prophets Isaiah, Jeremiah, and Zechariah. She is described by John in Revelation 17 as a prostitute, and an angelic interpreter tells John plainly: "The woman you saw is the great city that rules over the kings of the earth" (Revelation 17:18). It is a city of worldwide importance, a literal city that has been rebuilt for the last days.

> *The woman was dressed in purple and scarlet, and was glittering with gold, precious stones and pearls. She held a golden cup in her hand, filled with abominable things and the filth of her adulteries. This title was written on her forehead: Mystery, Babylon the Great, the mother of prostitutes and of the abominations of the earth.*
>
> REVELATION 17:4–5

This is also exactly how the prophet Zechariah described the future rebuilt city of Babylon. Zechariah was shown a woman representing the people's iniquity and "wickedness" (Zechariah 5:7–11). She would be carried to Shinar, or Babylon, and established again as the city embodying all evil. She is the "mother of prostitutes and of the abominations" because all the evil of the nations can be traced back to this one city, the first to defy God's authority.

Revelation 17 and 18 are similar. Both chapters say that Babylon, the "great city," is headed for devastation; both specify that she will be burned; and both name God as the ultimate source of her destruction.

In both chapters Babylon is described as a physical city, arrayed with "purple and scarlet" and "glittering with gold, precious stones and pearls." In both chapters the city possesses a cup. In both chapters Babylon commits fornication with the kings of the earth and causes all the nations of the earth to fall into a drunken stupor. In both chapters Babylon persecutes God's remnant who stand against evil.[2]

What has made Iraq different from, say Egypt, is a combination of Iraqi cultural pride, oil wealth, highly developed ideology, and Saddam Hussein's will to power. Even without him, the pride, potential wealth and probably the ideology would remain.

"We want to run things our own way," the soft-spoken Jabra said. "That is the Iraqi way."

JOHN YEMMA in the *Boston Globe*[3]

"Our own way" is the Babylonian way. Babylon was prideful, mirroring the excessive pride of her own Nebuchadnezzar. John writes that God declares, "Give her as much torture and grief as the glory and luxury she gave herself. In her heart she boasts, 'I sit as queen; I am not a widow, and I will never mourn'" (Revelation 18:7).

Iraqis willing to talk with Western reporters view the threat of war and economic hardship with a mixture of bravado and Arab fatalism. "We can live without Pepsi," bragged one Iraqi official. "Living in pride on dates and bread is much better than eating McKintosh [English candies] and drinking Pepsi."

San Jose Mercury News[4]

John writes that Babylon is remembered during the outpouring of the seventh bowl judgment. Only one Babylon, though, is mentioned.

> *God remembered Babylon the Great and gave her the cup*
> *filled with the wine of the fury of his wrath.*
> REVELATION 16:19

Immediately after this pronouncement, John recorded the destruction of "Babylon the Great," continuing the theme of its destruction through two chapters. And as Ladd has noted, "the first paragraph of chapter nineteen continues the celebration of the fall of Babylon and consists of a song of thanksgiving in heaven that God had judged the great harlot."[5]

> *After this I heard what sounded like the roar of a great multi-*
> *tude in heaven shouting:*
> *"Hallelujah! Salvation and glory and power belong to*
> *our God, for true and just are his judgments. He has con-*
> *demned the great prostitute who corrupted the earth by her*
> *adulteries. He has avenged on her the blood of his servants."*
> *And again they shouted:*
> *"Hallelujah! The smoke from her goes up for ever and ever."*
> REVELATION 19:1–3

The Pride of Man Is Cast Down

Babylon burns on the earth, and those in heaven rejoice.

Before her destruction, she was the "jewel of kingdoms, the glory of the Babylonians' pride" (Isaiah 13:19). But after her eradication, she becomes "a haunt for every evil spirit, a haunt for every unclean and detestable bird" (Revelation 18:2).

Desert creatures will lie there, jackals will fill her houses; there the owls will dwell, and there the wild goats will leap about. Hyenas will howl in her strongholds, jackals in her luxurious palaces.

ISAIAH 13:21–22

God's Conclusion to the "Tale of Two Cities"

We have identified and traced a biblical "tale of two cities" through the Bible: Babylon, the city chosen by man, and Jerusalem, the city chosen by God.

For a time in the conflict it appeared as though the city of man had won the struggle. Babylon threatened the land promised to Abraham's descendants and finally destroyed the kingdom of God on earth. The line of David was torn from the throne, and the city of Jerusalem was burned to the ground.

But God had other plans for both Babylon and Jerusalem. In the book of Revelation, John described two great cities:

Their bodies will lie in the street of the great city, which is figuratively called Sodom and Egypt, where also their Lord was crucified.

. . . Then there came flashes of lightning, rumblings, peals of thunder and a severe earthquake. No earthquake like it has ever occurred since man has been on earth, so tremendous was the quake. The great city split into three parts, and the cities of the nations collapsed. God remembered Babylon the Great and gave her the cup filled with the wine of the fury of his wrath.

REVELATION 11:8; 16:18–19

The first great city is Jerusalem. The lightning, thunder, and earthquake signal the end of the tribulation period. The great city of Jerusalem splits into three parts as the cities of the nations collapse. But the second great city is Babylon, a city great in its wickedness. As the time of God's judgment on the earth draws to a close, God remembers His vow to destroy Babylon the Great.

Babylon is destined for devastation, but Jerusalem is destined for deliverance. Babylon is the great prostitute; Jerusalem is "the bride, the wife of the Lamb" (Revelation 21:9). Babylon is dressed in purple and scarlet, glittering with gold, precious stones, and pearls; Jerusalem shines with the glory of God, and her brilliance is "like that of a very precious jewel, like a jasper, clear as crystal" (Revelation 21:11). Babylon rides upon a scarlet beast (Revelation 17:3), but Jerusalem comes "down out of heaven from God" (Revelation 21:10).

When God's final curtain falls on the world stage, only one of these cities will remain, and she will remain forever.

19
Scanning the Horizon

One night Christ led His disciples out from the beautiful temple of Herod and descended into the Kidron Valley. With the afternoon sun at their backs, they began the long climb up the Mount of Olives to the village of Bethany on the far side of the ridge. The disciples, gazing back at the temple and marveling at its size and beauty, behaved like gawking tourists as they gestured toward the building.

Jesus jarred their thoughts when He declared, "Do you see all these things? . . . I tell you the truth, not one stone here will be left on another; every one will be thrown down" (Matthew 24:2).

Christ's words of doom shocked the disciples. They assumed He was describing the times of trouble promised just prior to the establishment of God's kingdom on earth, and their thoughts churned as they continued their climb up the mountain. When they finally paused to rest, the disciples slipped to Jesus' side and quietly asked for more information. "Tell us . . . when will this happen, and what will be the sign of your coming and of the end of the age?" (Matthew 24:3).

Just like people today, the disciples wanted to know when the end times would come. They were also anxious to know the "signs of the times" that could help them discern the significance of world events.

Christ answered His disciples, and His words paint a picture of the time just prior to His second coming to earth. He stressed two points: First, no one should set a specific date.

> *"No one knows about that day or hour. . . . Therefore keep watch, because you do not know on what day your Lord will come. . . . So you also must be ready, because the Son of Man will come at an hour when you do not expect him."*
> MATTHEW 24:36, 42, 44

Date-setters will always be wrong. No individual can know the exact day or hour when God's future events will take place. It is unscriptural and unproductive to set a date. Besides, Christ instructs those who understand His message to "keep watch."

Christ's second point balances the first. No one will know exactly when God's prophetic clock will begin ticking, but we should expect God to begin arranging the stage for the final act of His drama. The stage may yet be empty of actors, but if all the props are in place and the houselights begin to dim, you can be sure the final act is soon to begin.

Christ expressed this idea by using a metaphor from the farmer's field:

> *"Now learn this lesson from the fig tree: As soon as its twigs get tender and its leaves come out, you know that summer is near. Even so, when you see all these things, you know that it is near, right at the door."*
>
> MATTHEW 24:32–33

The disciples could not know hours and days, but they could observe seasons. Just as the greening of the fig tree is a harbinger of summer, so the alignment of key nations and events could be the herald of God's final events.

Three Specific Signposts

What are the specific signposts that can serve as indications of God's end-time program for the world? I believe there are three.

First, the nation Israel must be in existence before the final seven-year time of trouble can begin on the earth. Since 1948 this signpost has been in place. Israel is the most crucial of the three signposts because she is at the center of God's end-time agenda.

God's second signpost is a revived Roman Empire.

A world power must reemerge from within the boundaries of the ancient Roman Empire. In Daniel 7 and Revelation 13, God indicates that this end-time power will take the form of a ten-nation confederacy that will exert political and military control over the rest of the world.

The Roman Empire occupied much of what today is Europe and the Mediterranean basin. Until the late 1980s it seemed impossible that this region could ever unite. The continent seemed hopelessly divided between NATO and Warsaw Pact forces—each poised to destroy the other. Within western Europe the Common Market had failed in its goal of uniting and strengthening the European community.

But then came the traumatic events of 1989 and 1990. Suddenly Europe entered a new era. The Cold War was over, the Warsaw Pact was dead, and the European Union forged ahead with plans for a strong, united Europe. Their common currency, the euro, already seeks to tie the nations together economically.

The second signpost is not yet in place, but we can watch the European political scene with interest. The Bible predicts that ten nations will unite. Together they will have tremendous military might and economic influence over the rest of the world. The inherent instability of various countries and cultures within the European Union will continue to pose problems, but this seems to match Daniel's description of the fourth empire as a hodgepodge of nations "so the people will be a mixture and will not remain united" (Daniel 2:43).

The third sure signpost is the rebuilding of Babylon. The city of rebellion where humanity first united against

God will again be the scene of the crime at the end of the ages. God allows wickedness to come full circle and end at the very spot where it began.

Modern excavations among the ruins of ancient Babylon began in the 1950s, but work was slow and little progress was made for nearly three decades. But after Saddam Hussein assumed absolute control of Iraq, the pace quickened. Work halted during the Gulf War, but it has since resumed.

Not only must Babylon exist; it also must serve as the capital of an economic empire that has a stranglehold on the world. Babylon will exert economic control over the revived Roman Empire and over "peoples, multitudes, nations and languages" (Revelation 17:15). Her influence will be worldwide.

The apostle John did not identify what would enable the city to exert so much power, but he predicted it would bring her incredible wealth. The "merchants of the earth will weep" when Babylon is destroyed "because no one buys their cargoes any more" (Revelation 18:11), and the sea captains will mourn their loss of income because "all who had ships on the sea became rich through her wealth" (Revelation 18:19).

Almost two thousand years after John wrote his remarkable predictions, we know what can bring such incredible wealth to this otherwise barren part of the globe. Oil! Black gold! A leader from Iraq will someday rule again from the city of Babylon. He will control the oil wealth of the Middle East, a whopping 50 percent of the proven oil reserves of the world! This one-man cartel will control the economic destiny of the West and will lavish much of his wealth on rebuilding his capital city of Babylon.

But at the end of this seven-year period, the world ruler from Europe will tire of the tactics of global blackmail being played by Babylon. Another multinational military force will travel to the Middle East. This force will enter Iraq from the northwest and attack from the north. Babylon and Iraq will be shattered.

After crushing Babylon, this world ruler will travel to Israel to finish off the country he has persecuted for three-and-a-half years. His armies will bivouac in the valley of Jezreel at the foot of the ancient tell of Megiddo in northern Israel. Here, at the "mountain of Megiddo" —Armageddon—the last great military campaign of this age will begin. The armies will fight their way to Jerusalem, Israel's final stronghold. Just when victory seems within the Antichrist's grasp, Jesus Christ will return from heaven with His hosts to destroy His adversaries and to begin His reign on earth. Then Israel will finally dwell safely in the land promised to Abraham.

What Does This Mean for You?

Three signposts, all pointing to the end times. When all three finally line up, the stage will be set for the most dramatic and deadly drama of all time. As we watch events in the Middle East unfold, it appears that these events could occur soon. What, then, ought to be our response?

Your response will depend on where you stand in relationship to God. God has stated plainly in the Bible that His ultimate desire for humanity is eternal life—life to the fullest both now and in eternity to come.

I have come that they may have life, and have it to the full.
JESUS CHRIST, in JOHN 10:10

One look at today's world and we realize that God's gift of eternal life to the fullest is a precious and rare commodity. The world is awash in bitterness, hatred, strife, wars, drugs, depression, and death. If God has such a lofty goal as full eternal life for this world, why are we mired in the muck, existing in a state of moral and ethical bankruptcy and turmoil?

The Bible states that our problem is sin: "For all have sinned and fall short of the glory of God" (Romans 3:23). We have consciously chosen to deviate from the standards laid down by God. A chasm has formed between humanity and God, and the gulf is too great to span through human effort.

Justice demands that those guilty of a crime ought to pay the consequences. We have violated God's standards, and the penalty for our violation is eternal death —separation from God now and for eternity. "For the wages of sin is death" (Romans 6:23).

Since the Flood humans have been building their own "towers of Babel," trying to find some way to reach heaven through their own efforts. We are in a never-ending search for a way to be fulfilled, happy, significant, or complete, but humanity's search always ends in a black abyss of despair. Isn't there a way to cross the chasm caused by sin and reach the fulfillment promised by God?

God Himself provided the solution for our dilemma.

"For God so loved the world that he gave his one and only Son, that whoever believes in him shall not perish but have eternal life."

JOHN 3:16

Sin requires payment, but God loved each of us so much that He sent His Son, Jesus Christ, to die in our place. When Christ died on the cross, He did so to pay the eternal penalty for the sins of all humanity. He died in your place to pay for your misdeeds. In effect, He became the bridge across the chasm separating us from God. God showed that Christ's payment was sufficient by allowing Him to rise from the dead.

Christ has provided the one and only way for us to cross over from the side of despair to the side of eternal life. Christ said, "I am the way and the truth and the life. No one comes to the Father except through me" (John 14:6).

On which side of this chasm are you? Are you still trying to build your own tower to heaven, to reach God on your own? Are you struggling through life looking for alternative ways to bridge the gap between your present life and the life you intuitively know should be possible?

This world isn't going to get any better, you know. If you have learned anything from this book, it is that God is bringing a time of unparalleled trouble on the earth in the coming days. While some are pointing to a new order of peace and prosperity, God's Word paints a picture of worldwide chaos, brutal warfare, environmental disasters, and economic collapse. Humanity is trying to build a tower to heaven, but that tower is about to collapse.

The good news is that today, right now, you can cross over from death to life by placing your trust for eternal life on what Jesus Christ has already done for you. Do you believe that when Jesus died on the cross, He died for your sins? Are you willing to trust Him for your eternal destiny—to place your life in His hands? If so, you can pray a simple prayer like the following:

Dear Lord, I know that my life is a mess and I'm separated from You. I also know and believe that You sent Your Son, Jesus Christ, to earth to die on the cross to pay the penalty for my sin. I now want to place my trust in Jesus Christ as the substitute for my sin. Please forgive me and give me eternal life. In Christ's name I ask this. Amen.

If you just prayed this prayer in sincerity, welcome to the other side of the chasm! You have passed from death to life. You are now a citizen of the heavenly city of Jerusalem where you will dwell with God for all eternity. But you don't have to wait until some future time to enjoy the benefits of eternal life. God can provide you with abundant life today.

Begin reading the Bible to find out what God can do in your life. I suggest that you begin reading the gospel of John to learn more about Jesus Christ. Start praying and sharing your deepest needs, fears, and desires with God. As your heavenly Father, He wants to hear from you. And join with a group of people who have also made a commitment to Christ. Let them help you learn to know Him better.

What Prophecy Means to the Believer

If you have already placed your trust in Christ, what can you do with what you've learned from this book? I believe God gives us insight into the future for three reasons.

We have hope in discouraging times. The world is drowning in discouragement and uncertainty. Whether people are talking about the economy, politics, the Middle East, terrorism, crime, drugs, or even the weather, most people feel as though they have lost control of their destiny. But God has given us glimpses of the future to remind us that He is in control.

Not only do we know what will happen on earth during the coming time of tribulation, but we know our personal destiny. Christians are the only people who can approach death with certainty and without fear, because God has revealed what it will be like on the other side of the grave. The God who is in control of the universe knows our every need. He is in control of everything, and because of His control we have hope: "We know that in all things God works for the good of those who love him, who have been called according to his purpose" (Romans 8:28).

We can stay pure in times of temptation. The world tries

to entice believers to buy into a bankrupt system. "It doesn't get any better than this!" "If it feels good, do it!" "Just do it!" How can believers fight off the temptation to make the pursuit of pleasure the major goal in life? After focusing on the cataclysmic changes God will bring on the earth, Peter offers an answer:

> *Since everything will be destroyed in this way, what kind of people ought you to be? You ought to live holy and godly lives as you look forward to the day of God and speed its coming. . . . So then, dear friends, since you are looking forward to this, make every effort to be found spotless, blameless and at peace with him.*
> 2 PETER 3:11–12, 14

It is easier to resist temptation when you know what your actions will ultimately bring. By describing both the destruction of earth and the glories of heaven, God motivates us to lay up treasures in heaven (Matthew 6:19–20) rather than live for earthly pleasures.

We are encouraged to share God's good news with others. Paul wrote the book of 2 Timothy from a prison cell. Knowing death was near, he wrote to encourage Timothy, who would face difficult days ahead. Paul based one of his most significant pleas not on current events, but on God's prophetic plan for the world. "In the presence of God and of Christ Jesus, who will judge the living and the dead, and in view of his appearing and his kingdom, I give you this charge: Preach the Word; be ready in season and out of season; correct, rebuke and encourage —with great patience and careful instruction. . . . Do the work of an evangelist" (2 Timothy 4:1–2, 5).

Paul knew that trouble was coming, but he looked beyond the immediate danger and saw the eternal destiny of the whole human race hanging in the balance. The chasm is fixed, but the way to cross over from death to life has been established through Christ's death. In light of God's future judgment of all humanity and in light of Christ's second coming, Paul urges Timothy to give as many people as possible the opportunity to hear God's good news of eternal life.

God's message of Babylon and Jerusalem, the biblical tale of two cities, is not a faint, forgotten cry. It is rather a window into the future for all who care to gaze ahead in time.

This message from God was not intended to fill the head, but to change the heart. If these events come to pass (and they will!), what difference should it make in your life? The answer to that question could well determine your eternal destiny.

Then a mighty angel picked up a boulder
the size of a large millstone
and threw it into the sea, and said:

"With such violence
the great city of Babylon will be thrown down,
never to be found again."

Revelation 18:21
THE BIBLE

Notes

CHAPTER ONE. BABYLON: RISING FROM THE ASHES OF TIME

1. John Burns, "New Babylon Is Stalled by a Modern Upheaval," *New York Times International*, October 11, 1990, A13.

CHAPTER TWO. A ROYAL MANDATE

1. Paul Lewis, "Nebuchadnezzar's Revenge: Iraq Flexes Its Muscles by Rebuilding Babylon," *San Francisco Chronicle*, April 30, 1989.

2. Antonio Caballero, "Rebuilding Babylon," *World Press Review*, February 1990, 74.

3. Rick MacInnes-Rae, "Saddam's Babylon," *CBC Radio*, August 2002.

4. Amy E. Schwartz, "Saddam Hussein's Babylon," *Washington Post*, April 4, 1990, A27.

5. Ibid

6. Michael Ross, "Can Babylon Relive Its Glory Days?" *Los Angeles Times*, January 16, 1987.

7. Lewis, "Nebuchadnezzar's Revenge."

8. Ross, "Can Babylon Relive Its Glory Days?"

9. Subhy Haddad, "Babylon Is Being Rebuilt to Lure Tourists and Build Iraqi Morale," *Philadelphia Inquirer*, October 10, 1986.

CHAPTER THREE. Why Rebuild Babylon?

1. Michael Ross, "Can Babylon Relive Its Glory Days?" *Los Angeles Times,* January 16, 1987.

2. C. S. Manegold and R. Wilkinson, "The Anchor and the Hope of the Weak and the Meek," *Newsweek,* August 13, 1990, 23.

3. Babylon (Baghdad: State Organization of Antiquities and Heritage, 1982).

4. Paul Lewis, *New York Times International,* April 19, 1989, 4Y.

5. Ibid

6. *Baghdad Observer,* September 23, 1987, 1.

7. Amy E. Schwartz, "Saddam Hussein's Babylon," *Washington Post,* April 4, 1990, A27.

8. Lewis, *New York Times International.*

9. *Baghdad Observer,* 2.

10. Babylon International Festival brochure for September 22, 1987.

11. John Burns, "New Babylon Is Stalled by a Modern Upheaval," *New York Times International,* October 11, 1990, A13.

12. Michael Elliott, "Not as Lonely as He Looks," *Time,* September 16, 2002, 36.

13. Muhammad Abd al-Fattah Muhsin, "The Attack Is Coming," *Al-Ahram,* September 23, 2002.

CHAPTER FOUR. Babylon's Rebellious Beginnings

1. Brown, Driver, and Briggs, *A Hebrew and English Lexicon of the Old Testament,* s.v. "*nimrod,*" 650.

2. H. L. Ellison, "Genesis 1–11," in *The International Bible Commentary,* ed. F. F. Bruce (Grand Rapids: Zondervan, 1986), 122–23.

3. William White, *Dictionary of Biblical Archaeology,* s.v. "Babylon, City of," 86.

4. D. J. Wiseman, *Nebuchadnezzar and Babylon* (London: Oxford Univ. Press, 1985), 68.

5. Gerhard von Rad, *Genesis: A Commentary,* revised ed. (Philadelphia: Westminster 1961), 149.

CHAPTER FIVE. A TALE OF TWO CITIES

1. Charles Dickens, *A Tale of Two Cities* (New York: Nelson Doubleday), 9.

2. Augustine, *City of God*.

3. James Monson, *The Land Between: A Regional Study Guide to the Land of the Bible* (Jerusalem: published by the author, 1983), 14.

4. For further reading, see the book of Hebrews, chapter 7.

CHAPTER SIX. JUDAH'S FOREIGN POLICY NIGHTMARE

1. Gerald Larue, *Babylon and the Bible* (Grand Rapids: Baker, 1969), 5.

2. Gerrit P. Judd, *A History of Civilization* (New York: Macmillan, 1966), 26.

3. This event is so significant it is also recorded in Isaiah 39:1–8 and 2 Chronicles 32:31.

4. Daniel David Luckenbill, ed., *The Annals of Sennacherib* (Chicago: University of Chicago Press, 1924), 24.

5. "Taylor Prism," in *Documents from Old Testament Times,* ed. D. Winton Thomas (New York: Nelson, 1958), 67.

6. 2 Kings 20:8–11 and 2 Chronicles 32:24.

CHAPTER SEVEN. TAINTED BY BABYLON

1. F. F. Bruce, *Israel and the Nations* (Grand Rapids: Eerdmans, 1963), 83.

2. J. B. Bury, S. A. Cook, and F. E. Adcock, eds., *Cambridge Ancient History,* 12 vols. (Cambridge: At the University Press, 1929), 3:209. The Egyptians had been sending forces to aid the Assyrians as early as 616 B.C. and had continued to do so until this battle in 609 B.C.

3. Donald J. Wiseman, *Chronicles of the Chaldean Kings (626–556 B.C.) in the British Museum* (London: Trustees of the British Museum, 1956), 67–69.

4. Wiseman, *Chronicles of the Chaldean Kings,* 71.

CHAPTER EIGHT. THE AGE OF CONFRONTATION

1. Donald J. Wiseman, *Chronicles of the Chaldean Kings (626–556 B.C.) in the British Museum* (London: Trustees of the British Museum, 1956), 73.

2. John Bright, *A History of Israel,* third ed. (Philadelphia: Westminster, 1981), 327.

3. Jeremiah 28:1–4, 10–11; 29:20–21.

4. Jeremiah 51:59.

5. William H. Shea, "Daniel 3: Extra-Biblical Texts and the Convocation on the Plain of Dura," *Andrews University Seminary Studies* 20 (Spring 1982): 29–52.

6. 2 Kings 25:1; Jeremiah 39:1; 52:4; Ezekiel 24:1.

7. Lamentations 2:20; 4:10; Ezekiel 5:10, 12.

8. Jeremiah 37:5.

9. Ezekiel 5:12.

10. Michael Dobbs, "Babylon Fights for New Reputation, Besmirched Long Ago," *San Jose Mercury News,* January 2, 1987, 5C.

CHAPTER NINE. HISTORY'S "HEAD OF GOLD"

1. See Daniel, chapter 4.

CHAPTER TEN. THE KING WHO ATE GRASS

1. Robert Koldewey, *The Excavations at Babylon,* trans. Agnes S. Johns (London: Macmillan, 1914), 11–12.

2. Koldewey, *Excavations,* 168.

3. A. K. Grayson, *Assyrian and Babylonian Chronicles, Texts from Cuneiform Sources* (Locust Valley, NY: J. J. Augustin, 1975), 109–10.

4. Opening remarks of Mr. Latif Nsayyif Jassim, Minister of Information and Culture, at the opening of the Babylon Festival (*Baghdad Observer,* September 23, 1987, 2).

5. Michael Dobbs, "Babylon Fights for New Reputation, Besmirched Long Ago," *San Jose Mercury News,* January 2, 1987, 5C.

6. Herodotus 1.191.

CHAPTER ELEVEN. CONQUERED BUT NOT DESTROYED

1. James B. Pritchard, *Ancient Near Eastern Texts Relating to the Old Testament,* 3d ed. (Princeton: Princeton University Press, 1969), 316.

2. A. K. Grayson, *Assyrian and Babylonian Chronicles, Texts from Cuneiform Sources* (Locust Valley, NY: J. J. Augustin, 1975), 110.

3. Pritchard, *Ancient Near Eastern Texts,* 316.

4. Herodotus 3.159.

5. Arrian *Anabasis of Alexander* 7.17.2.

6. Ibid., 7.19.4.

7. Strabo *Geography* 16.1.5.

8. Josephus *Antiquities of the Jews* 15.2.2.

9. Dio *Roman History* 68.30.1.

10. *Pausanias* 8.33.3.

11. M. N. Adler, "Benjamin of Tudela, Itinerary of," *Jewish Quarterly Review* 17 (1905): 514–30.

12. Tony Horwitz, "Paranoia Runs Deep in Iraqi Sands," *Washington Post,* November 20, 1988, E1.

13. Robert Koldewey, *The Excavations at Babylon,* trans. Agnes S. Johns (London: Macmillan, 1914), 11–12.

CHAPTER TWELVE. THE TWO TYRANTS

1. Marc Duvoisin, "Iraqi Leader Hussein Has Long Commanded Fear," *Philadelphia Inquirer,* August 3, 1990, A8.

2. Janet Cawley, "Hussein Doesn't Deny 'Butcher of Baghdad' Nickname," *Chicago Tribune,* August 3, 1990, 4C.

3. David Lamb, "The Line in the Sand," *Los Angeles Times,* November 25, 1990, 4T.

4. Ariel Sharon in an interview with Nathan Gardels, "Perspective on the Middle East," *Los Angeles Times,* November 6, 1990, 7B.

5. Sharon interview.

6. Faisal I quoted by Charles A. Radin, "Ancient Splits, Colonial Legacy Weigh on Iraq," *Boston Globe,* August 20, 1990, 4C.

7. Duvoisin, "Iraqi Leader Hussein."

8. Saddam Hussein quoted by David Lamb, "Saddam Hussein Held Hostage by His Obsession with the Arab Myth," *Los Angeles Times,* October 12, 1990, 14A.

9. President George W. Bush's comments to reporters at the White House, September 16, 2001.

10. "Iraq Rebuilds Babylon as Resistance Symbol," *Tampa Tribune Times,* September 27,1987, 10A.

11. *Baghdad Observer,* September 23, 1987, 2.

12. *From Nebuchadnezzar to Saddam Hussein, Babylon Rises Again* (Baghdad: Ministry of Information and Culture, Department of Information, 1990).

CHAPTER THIRTEEN. THE GRANDSON OF THE BABYLONIANS

1. Saddam Hussein quoted by David Lamb, "Saddam Hussein Held Hostage by His Obsession with the Arab Myth," *Los Angeles Times,* October 12, 1990, 14A.

2. Lamb, "Saddam Hussein Held Hostage."

3. Walter Laqueur, "Like Hitler, but Different," *Washington Post,* August 31, 1990, A25.

4. Carol Morello, "Iraqi Despot Seeks His Own Grand Era," *Philadelphia Inquirer,* June 29, 1990, A1.

5. Associated Press, "Firm Grip of Iraq's Hussein Lies Deep in Nation's Roots," *San Jose Mercury News,* March 10, 1987, 12D.

6. Daniel Williams, "The New King of Babylon?" *Los Angeles Times,* September 6, 1990, 7A.

7. Hussein quoted by Lamb, "Saddam Hussein Held Hostage."

8. John Barry, "What We Face: The Bottom Line," *Newsweek,* September 16, 2002, 32.

9. David Lamb, "The Line in the Sand," *Los Angeles Times,* November 25, 1990, 4T.

10. From David Lamb's reference to the Central Intelligence Agency's "The World Factbook 1990," The International Institute for Strategic Studies' "The Military Balance 1990–91," and The Center for Defense Information (*Los Angeles Times,* November 25, 1990, 4T).

11. Lamb, "The Line in the Sand."

12. Nick B. Williams Jr., "Buildup Will Force Some War-or-Peace Decisions," *Los Angeles Times,* November 13, 1990, 1A.

13. Lamb, "The Line in the Sand."

14. Lisa Beyer, "Siding with the U.S. Sheriff," *Time,* December 3, 1990, 70.

15. Lamb, "The Line in the Sand."

16. Ibid.

17. Ibid.

18. *Wall Street Journal,* January 8, 1990, A7.

19. Jane Bryant Quinn, "Iraq: It's the Oil, Stupid," *Newsweek,* September 30, 2002, 43.

20. Speech on the threat posed by Iraq presented by President George W. Bush at the Cincinnati Museum Center, Cincinnati, Ohio, October 7, 2002.

CHAPTER FOURTEEN. BABYLON TODAY: A CITY IN WAITING

1. John Burns, "New Babylon Is Stalled by a Modern Upheaval," *New York Times International,* October 11, 1990, A13.

2. Inscription at Babylon quoted by Daniel Williams, "The New King of Babylon?" *Los Angeles Times,* September 6, 1990, 7A.

CHAPTER FIFTEEN. BABYLON'S FALL FORETOLD

1. See Revelation 6:12–14; 8:5, 10, 12; 11:13, 19; 16:18–21.

2. See Daniel 7:23–25; Revelation 13:3–7; 17:8, 12–13.

3. See 2 Thessalonians 2:3–4.

4. See Revelation 13:14–17.

5. See Matthew 24:15–22.

6. See Revelation 19:11–21.

7. See 1 Thessalonians 4:13–17; Revelation 3:10.

8. One-fourth of 50 percent of 225 million equals 28.12 million people.

CHAPTER SIXTEEN. THE TIME OF THE LORD'S VENGEANCE

1. Robert Koldewey, *The Excavations at Babylon,* trans. Agnes S. Johns (London: Macmillan, 1914), 168.

2. See Jeremiah 31:31–34. Joel 2 and Ezekiel 36 picture this as the indwelling of the Holy Spirit in the life of the believer.

CHAPTER SEVENTEEN. BABYLON IN THE BOOK OF REVELATION

1. See Revelation 7:4–8.

2. See Revelation 11:1–2.

3. See Revelation 11:3–8.

4. See Revelation 12:1–17.

5. Michael Hirsley and Jorge Casuso, "Mideast Crisis Sparks Talk of Armageddon," *Chicago Tribune,* October 14, 1990, 1C.

6. Ferrell Jenkins, *The Old Testament in the Book of Revelation* (Grand Rapids: Baker, 1972), 22.

7. See Nehemiah 2:1–8 for the start of this time period.

8. See Matthew 21:1–11.

9. For an excellent presentation on the computation of this prophecy, see Harold Hoehner, *Chronological Aspects of the Life of Christ* (Grand Rapids: Zondervan, 1977), 115–39.

10. See Matthew 21:1–11 and Zechariah 9:9.

11. Jane Bryant Quinn, "Iraq: It's the Oil, Stupid," *Newsweek,* September 30, 2002, 43.

CHAPTER EIGHTEEN. THE SCENE IS SET

1. John Yemma, "Iraqis See the Future in the Past," *Boston Globe,* September 16, 1990, 1.

2. For a more detailed analysis of Revelation 17–18, see my two articles on the subject ("The Identity of Babylon in Revelation 17–18," two parts, *Bibliotheca Sacra* 144 [July–September 1987]:305–16; [October–December 1987]:433–49).

3. Yemma, "Iraqis See the Future in the Past."

4. Mercury News Wire Services, "Hardened Iraqis Take War Footing in Stride," *San Jose Mercury News,* September 4, 1990, 1A.

5. George E. Ladd, *A Commentary on the Revelation of John* (Grand Rapids: Eerdmans, 1972), 244.

SINCE 1894, Moody Publishers has been dedicated to equip and motivate people to advance the cause of Christ by publishing evangelical Christian literature and other media for all ages, around the world. Because we are a ministry of the Moody Bible Institute of Chicago, a portion of the proceeds from the sale of this book go to train the next generation of Christian leaders.

If we may serve you in any way in your spiritual journey toward understanding Christ and the Christian life, please contact us at www.moodypublishers.com.

"All Scripture is God-breathed and is useful for teaching, rebuking, correcting and training in righteousness, so that the man of God may be thoroughly equipped for every good work."
—*2 TIMOTHY 3:16, 17*

THE RISE OF BABYLON TEAM

ACQUIRING EDITOR:
Mark Tobey

BACK COVER COPY:
Julie-Allyson Ieron, Joy Media

COVER DESIGN:
Smartt Guys Design

INTERIOR DESIGN:
Ragont Design

PRINTING AND BINDING:
Dickinson Press Inc.

The typeface for the text of this book is
Berkeley